MOMENTS
of PEACE
for the
MORNING

PRESENTED TO

PRESENTED BY

DATE

MOMENTS *of* PEACE *for the* MORNING

MOMENTS *of* PEACE *for the* MORNING

BETHANYHOUSE
MINNEAPOLIS, MINNESOTA

Moments of Peace for the Morning
Copyright © 2005 by GRQ, Inc.
Brentwood, Tennessee

Published by Bethany House Publishers
11400 Hampshire Avenue South
Bloomington, Minnesota 55438

Bethany House Publishers is a division of Baker Publishing Group, Grand Rapids, Michigan.

ISBN-13: 978-0-7642-0169-1
ISBN-10: 0-7642-0169-7

Editor: Lila Empson
Associate Editor: Natasha Sperling
Writer: Jennifer Rosania
Design: Thatcher Design, Nashville, Tennessee

07 08 09   6 5 4 3

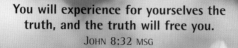

You will experience for yourselves the
truth, and the truth will free you.

JOHN 8:32 MSG

CONTENTS

Introduction

Good morning. Thank you for beginning your day with God.

Just as when you nourish your body with a hearty, healthy breakfast, feeding your soul with God's grace will renew and refresh you for the hours ahead. There is nothing that will affect your life in such a powerful and satisfying way as seeking God first thing in the morning.

These brief meditations have been fashioned to encourage you and give you hope. Some days, your faith will be reassured. Other days, you will be emboldened to live it out. Yet every morning you will experience the wonderful goodness of God.

Though it is impossible to describe the profound depth of God's love for you, you will grow to understand and appreciate it more as you spend time with your beloved Creator. He will empower you in difficult times, inspire you to meet challenges, and support you when you simply need to trust him. Undoubtedly, the Bible will guide you, his grace will comfort you, and his love will provide you with the strength to make it through the day.

God is waiting to fill you with joy and assure you that he is with you every step of your way.

Let the morning bring me word of your unfailing love, for I have put my trust in you. Show me the way I should go, for to you I lift up my soul.

PSALM 143:8 NIV

Moments of Peace for the Morning

The Lord God gives me the right
words to encourage the weary.
Each morning he awakens me
eager to learn his teaching.

ISAIAH 50:4 CEV

To Share His Love

In the beginning, God—who is limitless in power, wisdom, and love—wanted one thing. He wanted someone with whom to share his love. So he set about creating the universe.

> **In the beginning God created the heavens and the earth.**
> GENESIS 1:1 NLT

Words flowed from his mouth, forming planets and stars, continents and oceans. Yet as detailed and amazing as they were, they were only the stage for his dearest and best creation: you.

God created everything needed for you to live and for him to express his love to you. And he created you in his image—with a heart that could accept his love and reciprocate it.

God wants to share himself with you. Today, open your heart to him.

Dear God, thank you for creating such an amazing universe and for loving me. Help me to know your love and show you love in return. Amen.

Let them all praise the name of the LORD! He commanded, and they were created.

PSALM 148:5 GNT

God Understands

Some days you may feel that no one appreciates the unique pressures you face. And perhaps you are in such an exceptional situation that very few really could. God, however, knows you intimately and cares about what concerns you.

> **We do not have a High Priest who cannot sympathize with our weaknesses.**
> HEBREWS 4:15 NKJV

God knows the hidden thoughts of your heart and can see your circumstances from an all-encompassing viewpoint. He also knows how you feel when you are emotionally spent.

Always remember that God understands you very well—even better than you know yourself—and can help you overcome any challenge you face. Take heart today by trusting in him.

Dear God, thank you for understanding and loving me. Help me to always remember that—no matter what happens—you will help me through. Amen.

We are people of flesh and
blood. That is why Jesus
became one of us.

HEBREWS 2:14 CEV

Greeting the Savior

When Jesus entered Jerusalem during that last week of his life, the crowds welcomed him with palm branches and cheers. They happily greeted him as the answer to their hopes. They did not know that their joy would lie in the grave with him for three days. It was not until Jesus rose from the dead that they truly saw their hopes gloriously fulfilled.

> **Blessed is He who comes in the name of the LORD! Hosanna in the highest!**
> MATTHEW 21:9 NKJV

Today you may be disappointed that some exciting opportunities—things you praised God for—look like they've taken a turn for the worst. Yet continue to greet God with gladness. He will bring your dreams to life again in a way that will make you truly joyful.

Dear God, I greet you with joy. I praise you that no matter how it may look, you are breathing life into my dreams. Amen.

You make known to me
the path of life; in your
presence there is fullness
of joy; at your right
hand are pleasures
forevermore.

PSALM 16:11 ESV

The Delight of Blessing

God knew that what Abraham wanted most was a son—someone to love, teach, and carry on his name. Yet God wanted to do more than just provide Abraham with an heir—he wanted to give Abraham the joy of blessing others. So God made Abraham into a wonderful example of faith.

> **I will make of you a great nation, and I will bless you and make your name great, so that you will be a blessing.**
>
> GENESIS 12:2 ESV

God delights in providing your heart's desires as well. Yet he often allows you to wait because he wants you to be a blessing—and nothing blesses others more than a real, joyful trust that God works on behalf of those who love him.

Today, rejoice that God is making you a blessing to others. Your faith is delightful.

Dear God, thank you for blessing me. Strengthen my faith in your promises, and make me a joyful blessing to others. Amen.

Scripture foresaw that God would justify the Gentiles by faith and foretold the good news to Abraham, saying, All the nations will be blessed in you. So those who have faith are blessed with Abraham.

GALATIANS 3:8–9 HCSB

This Is Your Time

After the Babylonian captivity—when there were still Israelites in Persia—there arose an evil man named Haman who wanted to destroy the people of God. God—through various circumstances—placed Esther in King Xerxes' household, and she alerted him to Haman's plans. Esther trusted God, and God worked through her to save his people.

> **Who knows but that you have come to the kingdom for such a time as this and for this very occasion?**
> ESTHER 4:14 AMP

You can have peace today knowing that God has also placed you in your unique situation to have an extraordinary impact for him. He is not surprised at where you are. Rather, he put you there, gave you the gifts necessary for your circumstances, and will give you victory if you place your trust in him.

Dear God, I do trust you. Thank you for the peace of knowing that you are fulfilling a victorious plan in my circumstances. Amen.

We ask our God to make you worthy of the life he has called you to live. May he fulfill by his power all your desire for goodness and complete your work of faith.

2 THESSALONIANS 1:11 GNT

The Battle Belongs to God

The idea was to pit Israel's strongest warrior against the champion of the enemy. But even the bravest of Israel's soldiers were terrified of the mighty Goliath. That is, all except young David, who was there to deliver bread to his brothers. He knew that the battle wasn't about human strength; it was about the divine power of God.

> All this assembly shall know that the LORD does not save with sword and spear; for the battle is the LORD's.
>
> 1 SAMUEL 17:47 NKJV

This morning, are your thoughts on the Goliaths that challenge you today? If you are living for God, you can have triumphant confidence like David's, because no earthly threat can match the power of your heavenly champion. As you prepare for the day, trust him and relax. All your battles belong to God.

Dear God, thank you that I never have to fear the Goliaths in my life. I praise you for your power that wins every battle. Amen.

He had great success in everything he did because the LORD was with him.

1 SAMUEL 18:14 NCV

For the Right Moment

The excellent marksman does not waste his ammunition. He waits for the right opportunity and then sends his arrow flying at the precise moment for maximum effect.

> **In the shadow of His hand He has concealed Me; and He has also made Me a select arrow, He has hidden Me in His quiver.**
> ISAIAH 49:2 NASB

You are far too important to God for him to squander your talents or misplace you. In fact, you are so precious to him that he has hidden you close to him, to polish and perfect your spiritual gifts. He is waiting for the right moment—the right assignment—to send you soaring.

Today, be patient about what God is doing in you, and thank him for his timing and expertise. He has wonderful things for you to accomplish. Praise his name.

Dear God, it is hard to be patient, but I know I can trust your timing and skill. Thank you for your excellent assignments. Amen.

As for me, I trust in You, O LORD,
I say, "You are my God." My times
are in Your hand.

PSALM 31:14–15 NASB

Prepared, Not Forgotten

Isn't it wonderful that wheat is not ground forever? Eventually the milling process ends, and the grain is perfect for baking into bread.

As you awoke this morning, you may have felt like the grain—threshed and milled by trials. The moment will come, however, when the threshing ends, and you will be prepared with the patience, faith, and humility that only milling can create in your life.

> **Wheat is threshed and milled, but still not endlessly. The farmer knows how to treat each kind of grain.**
> ISAIAH 28:28 MSG

Just as the farmer knows what is required for each type of grain, God knows what preparation is essential for each person. He knows exactly what you need, so be patient and trust him.

Thank you, God, that trials don't last forever but that the qualities you build in me do. You are truly good to me. Amen.

This also comes from the LORD of hosts,
who is wonderful in counsel and
excellent in guidance.

ISAIAH 28:29 NKJV

Whatever He Wants

You never go wrong when you commit your way to God. He is always faithful to lead you in the very best way. And he promises that if you obey him he will protect you and cause you to prosper.

Sometimes his instructions will seem counterintuitive—very different from what you expected. And it will take real courage and faith to obey him because his instructions will not make sense from your standpoint. However, you can always be confident that God has excellent reasons for his commands—reasons of your protection and your prosperity.

> **Even if it isn't what we want to do. We will obey the LORD so that all will go well for us.**
> JEREMIAH 42:6 CEV

Take heart and commit to being faithful and obeying God today. You'll be glad you did.

Dear God, sometimes it is hard to obey, but I trust you to lead me well. Thank you that all of your commands are good. Amen.

Listen to and obey My voice, and I will be your God and you will be My people; and walk in the whole way that I command you, that it may be well with you.

JEREMIAH 7:23 AMP

No Way but Up

The four men heard that Jesus could do miracles, and a miracle was just what their paraplegic friend needed to be healed and to walk again. They carried him to where Jesus was staying.

Unfortunately, there were too many people for them to enter the house, and there was only one way for them to go—*up*. They transported their friend to Jesus by way of the roof, and they saw him miraculously healed because of their faith.

> **Amazement seized them all, and they glorified God and were filled with awe, saying, "We have seen extraordinary things today."**
>
> LUKE 5:26 ESV

You know people who are hurting as well. When you help them look up to Jesus, you see extraordinary things happen in their lives.

Today you'll meet people who really need Jesus. Show them the way up.

Dear God, I know that you love my hurting friends. Help me to show them how extraordinarily healing it is to look up. Amen.

At once the man got up in front of them all,
took the bed he had been lying on, and
went home, praising God.

LUKE 5:25 GNT

A Servant First

Some people decline to follow God because they are afraid that he will be an insatiable taskmaster. That is far different from how God has revealed himself in the Bible and throughout history. In fact, the greatest example of a humble servant is Jesus.

> **He came to serve, not to be served.**
> MARK 10:45 MSG

True, God asks for obedience. Yet he does so in order to free you to enjoy his blessings. He serves you by providing the peaceful, joyful, and fulfilling life you desire.

He will not answer the cries of your heart with fleeting remedies. He grows you in holiness and love so that you can experience the abundant life to the deepest degree.

Dear God, thank you for this abundant life. May I daily imitate you and humbly take part of your work in the world. Amen.

You have one Teacher, the Christ. The greatest among you will be your servant.

MATTHEW 23:10–11 NIV

A Letter of Recommendation

In Paul's time, false teachers forged letters of recommendation in order to establish their authority. Yet Paul declared that he needed no such letters, because whenever he taught about Jesus, changed human hearts confirmed God's approval and authority.

> **You are a letter of Christ, cared for by us, written not with ink but with the Spirit of the living God.**
> 2 CORINTHIANS 3:3
> NASB

God enables you to teach others about Jesus. Though theological training is useful, it is not as important as having a vibrant, living relationship with God, where his Spirit permanently writes on your heart.

You have his truth engraved within you. In fact, you are a letter of Christ. This morning, rejoice that it is a letter that many will be blessed in reading.

Dear God, thank you for teaching me deep within my heart by your spirit. May many read the letter you have written in me. Amen.

If you listen to constructive criticism,
you will be at home among the wise.

PROVERBS 15:31 NLT

The Words That Improve

Most people would agree that honesty is the best policy—unless it is honest criticism. That kind of candor is often difficult to take.

There are basically three ways people respond to criticism. One is to find fault with the messenger. Another is to internalize it so that it destroys their self-esteem.

> An honest answer is like a kiss on the lips.
> PROVERBS 24:26 NIV

The third way is to bring the criticism to God and ask him to reveal the truth in it. In this way, you allow him to teach you and reveal blind spots in your character that need work.

Today, remember that honesty really is an excellent policy—especially when it is accompanied by God's grace and truth.

Dear God, thank you that honest criticism doesn't have to hurt, but can truly improve me. Thank you for gently and lovingly teaching me your truth. Amen.

Let the words of Christ, in all their richness, live in your hearts and make you wise. Use his words to teach and counsel each other. Sing psalms and hymns and spiritual songs to God with thankful hearts.

Colossians 3:16 NLT

Receiving the Message

This morning, God is calling you to learn from him. He whispers that he loves you and that you can trust him. He tells you that when you think there is no help for you, he will rescue you.

He encourages you to be strong because he vindicates you and never lets you be dishonored. He says that his wisdom, power, and love have worked together to provide good plans for your life.

> **The LORD God gives me the right words to encourage the weary. Each morning he awakens me eager to learn his teaching.**
> ISAIAH 50:4 CEV

He also wants you to know that he has comforted you in order to prepare you to encourage others. His words can give life and hope to the weary, if only you will receive and share them.

Dear God, I do receive your words today. Thank you for such profound promises. Help me to share them with whoever needs them. Amen.

Who among you fears the LORD and obeys the voice of his servant? Let him who walks in darkness and has no light trust in the name of the LORD and rely on his God.

ISAIAH 50:10 ESV

Moments of Peace
for the Morning

This is eternal life, that they know you
the only true God, and Jesus Christ
whom you have sent.

JOHN 17:3 ESV

Knowing Him Is Eternal

There will be times in your life when your only source of comfort will be God. It will be through worship, prayer, and Bible study that you gain the energy, wisdom, and hope to make it through the day.

This is not a trial, this is the goal—to need no earthly encouragement because God has become everything to you. Your comfort, peace, and joy all come from God. It is during these times that God replaces your earthly nature with a love and longing for the eternal.

> **This is eternal life, that they know you the only true God, and Jesus Christ whom you have sent.**
> JOHN 17:3 ESV

Rejoice. God is preparing you for eternal life by changing your perspective and helping you to know him better.

I thank you, God, that learning about you today is about loving you in countless tomorrows. I love you and praise your wonderful name. Amen.

Build yourselves up in your most holy faith;
pray in the Holy Spirit; keep yourselves in
the love of God, waiting for the mercy of
our Lord Jesus Christ that leads
to eternal life.

JUDE 1:20–21 ESV

Asking for Help

Though Moses believed he should mediate the people's disputes, it was just too much for him to handle—the line of aggravated Israelites was endless. His father-in-law gave him this excellent advice: Find capable people to share the responsibilities—people who could do the job if something happened to him.

> **Appoint some competent leaders who respect God and are trustworthy and honest.**
> EXODUS 18:21 CEV

You don't have to handle everything by yourself either. In fact, it is not only acceptable for you to get help, but it is also part of God's plan for training others to do his work. In this way you relieve your own burden while blessing someone else with a ministry.

Find reliable people to mentor today, and enjoy watching them grow.

Dear God, help me to be humble enough to ask for help in my responsibilities so that others can learn to serve you. Amen.

These judges can handle the ordinary cases and bring the more difficult ones to you. . . . You won't be under nearly as much stress, and everyone else will return home feeling satisfied.

EXODUS 18:22–23 CEV

Of Disciplines and Victories

Just as determination and physical discipline go hand in hand for athletes, so faith and a spiritually consistent life work together for you who believe in God.

Athletes train their bodies daily and observe the rules because victory is their goal. Without the goal, there is no reason to train. Without training, they will not achieve their goal.

Like the athlete, you exercise your spiritual muscles through prayer, Bible study, and obedience to God. These disciplines make your faith in God's promises stronger and bring you closer to the prize of knowing God. The spiritual disciplines work together to bring you the victory.

> **If anyone competes as an athlete, he does not win the prize unless he competes according to the rules.**
>
> 2 Timothy 2:5 NASB

Dear God, starting today, help me to have a consistent spiritual life that builds strong faith — and the strong faith that motivates a godly life. Amen.

I press on toward the goal
for the prize of the upward
call of God in Christ Jesus.

PHILIPPIANS 3:14 NASB

Living in the Light

As the sun rises this morning, it is easy to see why light is a blessing—it is essential for sight and growing things. Yet spiritual light is even more amazing because it produces goodness, righteousness, and truth.

> **Christ will give you light.**
> EPHESIANS 5:14 NKJV

Jesus illuminates your life. He sees the good you do in secret and celebrates it with you. His radiance heals the areas of hurt hidden deep within you that prevent you from growing. And he brightens your way with hope whenever the road ahead seems dark.

Jesus is your light. And as he illuminates your life, he kindles your goodness, grows you in righteousness, and lights your way with truth.

Dear God, thank you for the beautiful light of Jesus that helps me to grow and to see as you do. My life is hopeful and bright because of you. Amen.

[You are] light in the Lord. Walk as children of light for the fruit of the light [results] in all goodness, righteousness, and truth.

EPHESIANS 5:8–9 HCSB

The Fabric of the Everlasting

Wrap yourself in this beautiful promise today—God's love is always, constantly, and ceaselessly with you. His love adorns you with salvation, protection, guidance, and provision. It shrouds you from your cold, piercing fears.

Nothing can reach you, except that which is allowed by his covering grace.

> From everlasting to everlasting the LORD's love is with those who fear him.
> PSALM 103:17 NIV

Though you may lay his love aside and get far away from him in your own heart, he remains close by.

He weaves himself intimately into your life so that nothing can separate his eternal cords from your earthly cloth. Joyfully wear the love of God forever.

Dear God, how great and steadfast is your love. Dress me in it this morning, and my heart will sing your praises forever. Amen.

As God's chosen people, holy and dearly
loved, clothe yourselves with compassion,
kindness, humility, gentleness and patience.
COLOSSIANS 3:12 NIV

It Was Very Good

God is at work in you. The fact that you awoke this morning with a desire for a word from him demonstrates his activity. In opening his word and praying, you welcomed him into your life to continue forming you into a good, useful instrument.

He is constantly drawing and teaching you—making you ready for good works that are uniquely suited to you. Though you may feel useless or unworthy, he sees what pleases him—what he deems as very, very good.

> **God looked over everything he had made; it was so good, so very good!**
> GENESIS 1:31 MSG

He is readying you for great endeavors. Rejoice that God is proud of you and has deemed you worthy of being his choice instrument for important assignments to come.

Dear God, thank you for working in my life and for doing good things in me and through me. May I truly be a useful instrument. Amen.

We are God's workmanship, created in Christ Jesus to do good works, which God prepared in advance for us to do.

EPHESIANS 2:10 NIV

The Delight of Creating

God takes joy in creating. He loves inventing worlds of delight for you.

First, he plants a desire in you—a seed that he lovingly nurtures. Undoubtedly, some special hope comes to mind. You know that it originated with him because it is impossible to achieve without him. You know that when it is accomplished, he will receive all the glory and praise.

> **The LORD made the heavens and everything in them by his word.**
> PSALM 33:6 CEV

Then, he creates conditions for that hope to mature and blossom. He delights in growing it into something that is above and beyond what you could imagine. And he loves to see your joyous face when you finally grasp the delightful things he created just for you.

Dear God, you are my joy. Just as you created the world by your word, I know you are powerfully inventing good things for me. Amen.

Delight yourself also
in the Lord, and He
will give you the
desires and secret
petitions of your
heart.

PSALM 37:4 AMP

The Name of Joy

Many people believe that the phrase "God helps them that help themselves" is in the Bible. However, it was actually written by Benjamin Franklin.

There are issues in which you cannot help yourself. There are hurts you do not know how to heal, mistakes you need forgiveness for, and obstacles to knowing God that you are unable to overcome by yourself.

> **You are to name Him Jesus, because He will save His people from their sins.**
> MATTHEW 1:21 HCSB

God brings you joy because he prevails over *all* those things. Your victory is not about how hard you try but about how he helps you.

God has done extraordinary things for you—even providing the way for you to know God. His is the name of joy—say it today with gladness.

Dear God, your name makes me rejoice. Thank you for doing everything necessary so that I can enjoy you forever. Amen.

We can rejoice in our wonderful new relationship with God—all because of what our Lord Jesus Christ has done for us in making us friends of God.

ROMANS 5:11 NLT

In His Hands

When the Israelites went into captivity, God promised that it would not last forever. He assured them that they would someday return to their homeland.

God eventually moved King Cyrus's heart to send them back to Jerusalem and give them the resources needed to rebuild the city.

> The king's heart is like channels of water in the hand of the LORD; He turns it wherever He wishes.
>
> PROVERBS 21:1 NASB

God's ability to help you is absolutely limitless. All things concerning your situation—including the hearts of people in authority over you—are in his hand. You may not be able to influence the people who could change your circumstances, but God certainly can and will.

Take peace this morning knowing that he is directing your situation like a watercourse and is helping you mightily.

Dear God, thank you that the hearts of the people who could help me are in your hands. The ways you help me are truly limitless. Amen.

I will raise up Cyrus in
my righteousness: I will
make all his ways
straight. He will rebuild
my city and set my
exiles free.

Isaiah 45:13 NIV

None Other Beside Him

As Israel prepared to claim the Promised Land, God reminded them of the great miracles he had done to rescue them from Egypt. No obstacle impeded him—not Pharaoh's army, not the Red Sea, or not even the lack of food and water in the wilderness. God did it all so that Israel would acknowledge him as God and have confidence in him.

> **To you it was shown, that you might realize and have personal knowledge that the Lord is God; there is no other besides Him.**
> DEUTERONOMY 4:35
> AMP

God sometimes gives you obstacles as well—to build your trust in his love and power. Today, acknowledge that he is God and there is no other worthy source of help beside him. Go to him with your troubles, and be confident that he will care for you.

Dear God, you did wondrous things for Israel, and you've done amazing things for me. Truly, you are worthy of praise. Amen.

The Lord brought us out of Egypt
with a strong hand and . . . signs
and wonders. He led us to this
place and gave us this land, a land
flowing with milk and honey.

DEUTERONOMY 26:8–9 HCSB

As Soon as You Prayed

Often it is in the early morning hours when you are reminded of your most cherished, private prayers. The thought flickers in your mind, *Is today the day that God answers me? Will I see my deepest longing fulfilled?*

> God thinks highly of you, and at the very moment you started praying, I was sent to give you the answer.
> DANIEL 9:23 CEV

God's response to you is the same as the angel reported to Daniel—at the very moment you started praying, he began to answer.

You may see God's answer today, but be encouraged even if you don't. Be assured that God has heard your prayer and has sent his mighty power and provision in response to it. His help is on the way. Trust him—his answers are always right.

Dear God, thank you so much for answering my prayer. Though I may not see your provision today, I praise you that it is definitely coming. Amen.

**God answered their prayers
because they trusted him.**
1 Chronicles 5:20 MSG

A Long March

The Israelites were instructed to march once around Jericho for six days—and seven times around on the seventh day. Finally they were to shout, and the city's walls would fall.

> **Shout, for the LORD has given you the city!**
> JOSHUA 6:16 NKJV

The weary Israelites were probably dubious about the instructions. However, they obeyed God and shouted out in faith—confident that he had already conquered Jericho.

God has given you Jerichos as well—strongholds that you've wanted to conquer. You trust God's promises, but you're exhausted from such a long march.

This morning, you must shout. Loudly proclaim that God has fulfilled his pledge. Express your faith that the march is nearly done—and that triumph is already yours.

Dear God, it has been a long, tiring march, but I shout out in praise that you've already won. Thank you for the coming success. Amen.

Their strength and weapons were not what won the land and gave them victory! You loved them and fought with your powerful arm and your shining glory.

PSALM 44:3 CEV

His Treasure

The tender words of the Shepherd paint a beautiful picture of seeking out and finding a lost lamb, one he cares for and loves.

God seeks you out as well. Not only for salvation—though that is the most important reason—but to care for you.

> **Rejoice with me, because I have found my sheep which was lost.**
> LUKE 15:6 AMP

He searches the areas of your life where you are distant from him—the areas of pain that you fear showing him—so he can protect you from danger and heal your wounds.

When you feel lost, afraid, or alone, God is right there for you. And he rejoices when you return to him, because you are his treasure—truly valuable and loved.

This morning, praise God that he is your treasure as well.

Dear God, this morning I thank you for treasuring me. I cherish you and commit myself to discovering just how priceless you are. Amen.

Where your treasure is, there will your heart be also.

LUKE 12:34 AMP

Of God or Men?

It is difficult to watch people you love choose courses that are fraught with challenges or experience a very painful trial. Sometimes you will not understand what God is doing in them, and you will want to safeguard them from experiencing distress.

> **You are not setting your mind on God's interests, but man's.**
> MATTHEW 16:23 NASB

God may have an important purpose for their circumstances that you are not aware of.

It is okay when you do not comprehend what God is doing. Today, do not shield your loved ones from trials. Rather, pray for and support them.

By doing so, you observe God's interests as well as theirs.

Dear God, I pray for my hurting loved ones. Thank you for doing important things in their lives. Please show me how to encourage them. Amen.

There you shall be rescued; there the LORD will redeem you. . . . But they do not know the thoughts of the LORD; they do not understand his plan.

MICAH 4:10, 12 ESV

Moments of Peace for the Morning

"Not by might nor by power, but by my Spirit," says the Lord Almighty.

ZECHARIAH 4:6 NIV

Humbly Accepting His Teaching

It is truly marvelous when God answers your prayers and fulfills the promises you've waited so long for. Though you know that everything is possible with God, his work is transformed from an intellectual fact to a deep peace within you. Faith fills your heart.

> **I will instruct you and teach you in the way you should go.**
> PSALM 32:8 ESV

God is teaching you. You realize that he was guiding you when the path seemed strange; he was working when you couldn't see his hand.

God teaches you as much when he fulfills his promise as while you're waiting. This morning, accept his direction. When you look back, you'll see how he adjusted your path and how today's obedience was integral to tomorrow's blessings.

Dear God, I look forward to following your instruction today. Thank you for guiding me in the way I should go. Amen.

I pay careful attention as you lead me, and I follow closely. As soon as you command, I do what you say.

PSALM 119:59–60 CEV

Choosing the Influence

What influences you? From where do you receive information? Psalm 1 draws an interesting distinction between people who chase after temporary things and those who look to God.

It may seem appropriate to study the newest techniques or listen to the latest guru to help you accomplish your goals. However, though some of their strategies may have some value, they will not have the enduring results that God promises.

> **The Law of the LORD makes them happy, and they think about it day and night.**
> PSALM 1:2 CEV

Meditate on the Bible and drink in the principles that nourish your soul and help you find success. Your accomplishments will not be based on earthly things that pass away, but on a lasting foundation that is eternal.

Dear God, I choose you as my influence and meditate on the Bible. Thank you for accomplishing wonderful, eternal things through me. Amen.

They are like trees growing beside a stream, trees that produce fruit in season and always have leaves. Those people succeed in everything they do.

PSALM 1:3 CEV

By His Spirit

As you awoke this morning, what was on your mind? Was it the challenges you will face today? Are there problems you need to confront—issues that are too massive for you to handle?

God knows everything that concerns you today. And though you may not be able to conquer the difficulties on your own, God strengthens and enables you to face them by his Spirit.

> "Not by might nor by power, but by my Spirit," says the Lord Almighty.
>
> Zechariah 4:6 NIV

You don't have to rely on your own strength and wisdom; God provides his boundless resources to you. No matter what is ahead today, take heart. You will be amazed by what you can accomplish when your work is empowered by God's Spirit.

Dear God, thank you that the things ahead today are conquerable by your Spirit. Thank you for giving me your strength and wisdom. Amen.

I'm filled with God's power, filled with
God's Spirit of justice and strength.
MICAH 3:8 MSG

A Better Perspective

Are there people in your life with whom you have a conflict? Do you have expectations of how they will react to you when you see them?

Whether those expectations are positive or negative, your responsibility is to love those people and honor them above yourself.

> **Love each other as brothers and sisters and honor others more than you do yourself.**
> ROMANS 12:10 CEV

The apostle Paul did so by trying to understand other people's points of view. He knew if he could see from their perspective, he could better represent Christ to them.

Expect the best of those people when you see them today, and give them the benefit of the doubt. Not only will you have a better perspective about them, you will better represent Christ.

Dear God, help me to see things from other people's perspective so that I can truly represent you well when I see them today. Amen.

I entered their world and tried to experience things from their point of view. I've become just about every sort of servant there is in my attempts to lead those I meet into a God-saved life.

1 Corinthians 9:22 MSG

Paul, a Prisoner

Paul had been telling people about Jesus. This angered the religious leaders, and they had him arrested. Undoubtedly, those who had been blessed by his ministry were heartbroken. What a shame that this great man had been imprisoned—prevented from doing God's work.

> **I, Paul, am a prisoner for the sake of Christ.**
> PHILEMON 1:1 MSG

Or was he? Paul did not waste the time God had given him as a prisoner. He wrote letters to encourage the churches. And those letters—now a vital, irreplaceable part of the New Testament—have encouraged churches and taught Christians throughout the ages.

Paul's work was more meaningful than even he could have imagined. Remember that the next time you feel locked away by circumstances. God has an eternal purpose for putting you where you are.

Dear God, this morning I thank you that in every real and symbolic prison, you are still working out your wonderful will. Amen.

We continually
remember before our
God and Father your
work produced by
faith, your labor
prompted by love,
and your endurance
inspired by hope in
our Lord Jesus Christ.

1 THESSALONIANS 1:3 NIV

Wholehearted Work

God allows situations in your work and life that will make no sense to your dreams—aspirations that you thought had come from him. Nevertheless, God instructs you to carry on as if working for him, rather than dwelling on your circumstances. That is because it is through those situations that he becomes your central focus, and you learn to cling to him above all other things—including your ambitions.

> **Whatever you do, do your work heartily, as for the Lord rather than for men.**
> COLOSSIANS 3:23 NASB

Today, take heart that as long as you serve God, you are doing exactly as you are supposed to. Even if you lack work, he has assignments for you to accomplish. Someday soon, he will restore your dreams in a powerful way.

Dear God, thank you for my situation—even though it is confusing to me. I will work wholeheartedly for you. Please bless the work of my hands. Amen.

I would rather be a doorkeeper in the house of my God than dwell in the tents of wickedness . . . No good thing will He withhold from those who walk uprightly.

Psalm 84:10–11 NKJV

A Courageous Life

Sometimes you will have an immense longing for heaven. To be free of suffering, fear, illness, debt, heartbreak, and stress would be just . . . well, heavenly.

This was Paul's condition in prison. His greatest joy was thinking about being with Jesus in heaven—free from persecution and pain. Yet until God called him home, he was determined to live in a manner that honored Christ.

> I . . . hope that I will in no way be ashamed, but will have sufficient courage so that now as always Christ will be exalted.
> PHILIPPIANS 1:20 NIV

It takes courage to live as a Christian—to face challenges by redirecting your focus from your weaknesses to God's strength. Yet that is what you have been called to do. And you can do it. You can live courageously today. And God will certainly be exalted in you.

Dear God, I want to live in a way that honors you. Give me the courage to look past my problems to your power. Amen.

Live in a way that brings honor to the Good News of Christ . . . standing strong with one purpose, that you work together as one for the faith of the Good News.

PHILIPPIANS 1:27 NCV

The Defender Sees

You will occasionally find yourself in situations in which you cannot defend yourself. You may be required to remain quiet in the face of others saying erroneous thing about you. Or perhaps you will face the consequences of another's decisions; though you know the folly of their actions, you are not in a position to question what they are doing.

> **Nothing is concealed that will not be revealed, or kept secret that will not become known.**
> MATTHEW 10:26 AMP

This morning, take heart. Remember that God knows everything about your situation and that he is in control. Be confident that he will defend you when you can't speak up for yourself and that he will bring the truth to light. He knows the good you've done and will not let you down.

Dear God, thank you for caring about me. You are my great defender, and I know that you will bring the truth to light. Amen.

Wake up! Come and defend me! My God and Lord, fight for me! LORD my God, defend me with your justice. Don't let them laugh at me.

PSALM 35:23–24 NCV

Growing Closer With Forgiveness

Asking for forgiveness required humility, but the sinful woman was well aware of her neediness. She also knew that only Jesus could give her what she most wanted—relief from her guilt. As she wiped his feet with her tears, she received something unexpected—her heart began to overflow with love.

> Her sins, which are many, have been forgiven, for she loved much.
> LUKE 7:47 NASB

You grow closer to God when you receive his forgiveness. When you allow him to heal your deepest guilt, the freedom he gives produces a great spring of love in you. And that love results in profound worship.

This morning, experience his forgiveness and the wonderful overflow of his love.

Dear God, please forgive my sin. Thank you for giving me freedom so that I can grow closer to you and experience your wonderful love. Amen.

O Lord, you are so good, so ready
to forgive, so full of unfailing
love for all who ask your aid.

Psalm 86:5 NLT

Practice and Perfection

Love is a gift from God that must be used in order to be useful. The more you love others, the more your capacity to love will grow. The more you sacrifice for others, the more deeply you will care for all people.

> **If we love each other, God lives in us, and his love has been brought to full expression through us.**
> 1 JOHN 4:12 NLT

You also have the wonderful promise that if you love others, God—the source of love—lives in you. The more you practice his unfailing love, the more his presence is perfected in you.

The blessing of love is twofold. Love others, and not only will your love grow, but God—the spring from which all love flows—will show himself more powerfully within you.

Dear God, thank you for your loving presence. Help me practice being loving toward others so that your love is fully expressed through me. Amen.

May the Lord make your love for each other and for everyone else grow by leaps and bounds.

1 THESSALONIANS 3:12 CEV

What Grows From Your Tears

Sometimes the tears just flow. Burdens get so heavy and decisions so difficult that your natural response is to weep.

> **He who goes out weeping, bearing the seed for sowing, shall come home with shouts of joy, bringing his sheaves with him.**
> PSALM 126:6 ESV

God knows the tears you have cried, and he honors every one of them by transforming them into seeds of hope. He produces a harvest of virtues within you—righteousness, humility, faith, and perseverance all grow from your weeping.

Rejoice that your tears are not in vain. God cultivates each glistening drop and transforms it into a blessing. When you see what God has done in you and how he has worked in your situation, you will also have a harvest of truly unshakeable joy.

Dear God, I praise you that one day I will shout with joy over the harvest of virtues you have produced from my tears. Amen.

Our mouths filled with laughter, and our tongues with singing. Then they said among the nations, The Lord has done great things for them.

PSALM 126:2 AMP

Exalt Him

God is exalted above all of creation. He is the King of kings—the mighty sovereign of everything that exists. He is the Lord of lords—the able protector and provider for all he surveys.

He deserves your praise. His goodness and love are like a never-ending spring quenching your thirst. His holiness and wisdom bring joy to your heart. There is nothing too difficult for your God—and no good thing he would withhold from you.

> **Honor and majesty surround him; strength and beauty are in his dwelling.**
> 1 CHRONICLES 16:27 NLT

Exalt God today with your praise, and call to him whenever you are overwhelmed. He can overcome any problem you have, and thoroughly delights in your songs of trust.

My God and my King, you are beautiful in my sight. I praise you for your holiness and strength. Thank you for loving me. Amen.

Make a joyful noise to the Lord, all you lands! Serve the Lord with gladness! Come before His presence with singing!

PSALM 100:1–2 AMP

A Heavenly Accord

An important truth is that *God accepts you.*
His acceptance began in heaven with his
desire to have a relationship with you. He
provided the way to have
that relationship through
Jesus, and the communi-
cation that keeps the relationship healthy through
his Holy Spirit. God made
it possible for you to be
united with him in peace.

> **God . . . sent Christ to make peace between himself and us, and he has given us the work of making peace between himself and others.**
> 2 CORINTHIANS 5:18
> CEV

Tell people. Today,
tell others of how God has
done wondrous things to
show how he accepts you—and them too. It is
a heavenly accord they will want to be in on.

*Dear God, thank you for making peace between
us. I look forward to sharing that peace
with others today. Amen.*

God was in Christ, offering peace and
forgiveness to the people of this world.
And he has given us the work of sharing
his message about peace.

2 CORINTHIANS 5:19 CEV

A Unique Peace

Peace, by the world's standard, is defined by absence of conflict and achieved by abundance of strength. It is easy to assume that you should only go to God when you are strong or on your best behavior.

You don't have to be tough or without troubles in order to have peace. God gives you peace when you feel tired and weak—even when you've failed. That is because it is when you are vulnerable that you are truly receptive to him.

> My peace I give you. I do not give to you as the world gives. Do not let your hearts be troubled and do not be afraid.
> JOHN 14:27 NIV

God gives you perfect, unfaltering peace through the protective power of the Holy Spirit. This morning, rest calmly in the strength of God.

Dear God, thank you for the unique peace you give to those who trust in you. I will not be afraid knowing you protect me. Amen.

The LORD will give strength to His people;
The LORD will bless His people with peace.

PSALM 29:11 NKJV

Moments of Peace for the Morning

My peace I give you. I do not
give to you as the world gives.
Do not let your hearts be
troubled and do not be afraid.

JOHN 14:27 NIV

Encouraged and Hopeful

True hope is hard won. It begins with the daily pressures you face. Through them, you grapple with the truth of God—who he is and what he has promised.

Pressures produce perseverance—the ability to keep going and be patient because you see that God has never let you down. And that perseverance produces character, because your life is not based on daily changes but on God's eternal truth.

> **Hope does not disappoint, because the love of God has been poured out within our hearts through the Holy Spirit.**
> ROMANS 5:5 NASB

That truth produces hope, which does not disappoint because you have seen his goodness.

Through it all you know him and love him more and that is truly a reason to feel encouraged and hopeful.

Dear God, today I praise you for pouring out your love and giving me hope. Even in the daily pressures, you are doing wonderful things. Amen.

Let us rejoice and exult in our
hope of experiencing and
enjoying the glory of God.

ROMANS 5:2 AMP

Unchanging Heavenly Light

One of God's wonderful attributes is that he does not change—which is why you can have absolute confidence in him and patiently wait for whatever he has promised you.

God has never misled anyone, and he has never failed to fulfill his promises. Though sometimes he will allow you to wait in order to build your faith, his promise remains sure.

> **I am GOD—yes, I AM. I haven't changed.**
> MALACHI 3:6 MSG

Just as he faithfully gave Abraham, Joseph, and David their hearts' desires after they had waited, he will do the same for you.

Be patient, and let this truth light your way when it seems dark. God has not changed his mind concerning you—and he never will.

Dear God, this is the light I keep for the dark times—you never change. Thank you for the promises that you are perfecting for me. Amen.

Every good gift and every perfect gift is from above, coming down from the Father of lights with whom there is no variation or shadow due to change.

JAMES 1:17 ESV

Out of the Deep

Difficult days come unexpectedly—like a flood. You cannot plan for them; neither can you prepare for how they affect you. Though outside, unexpected forces may be their cause, they mainly come through the common things of life. It is the abundance of small, daily problems that can inundate your soul.

> He reached down from on high and took hold of me; He pulled me out of deep waters.
> 2 Samuel 21:17 HCSB

Even as the waters of adversity rage, remember that God is your great lifeguard and that he is able to rescue you. Turn each problem—each drowning drop of difficulty—over to him this morning. Surely he will lift you out of the overwhelming waters and bring you out to a spacious place where you can breathe.

Dear God, thank you for rescuing me out of any deep wave of difficulty that comes my way. I truly delight in you. Amen.

He brought me out to a wide-open place;
He rescued me because He delighted in me.

2 SAMUEL 21:20 HCSB

When Others Seek Your Kindness

As the great army of Israelites advanced across the Promised Land, word spread about the mighty, powerful God who helped them conquer every foe.

> **Please promise me in the LORD's name that you will be as kind to my family as I have been to you.**
>
> JOSHUA 2:12 CEV

Many—understanding that the Israelites served the one true God—pledged their help and allegiance in return for the Israelites' assurance of kindness and safety.

Today, you will meet with people who will see God's power in you and realize there is something very special about the God you serve. They may even ask you questions.

Be kind to them and tell them about the great God who has shown you such profound love. They will find safety in him, and will surely appreciate your helpfulness.

Dear God, may your goodness shine in me so others will see how wonderful you are and seek your kindness and security. Amen.

Have reverence for Christ in your hearts, and honor him as Lord. Be ready at all times to answer anyone who asks you to explain the hope you have in you.

1 PETER 3:15 GNT

A Work of His Hands

This morning, are you pondering what God is doing in your life? You may not know, and that is okay. However, the real question is this: Do you have confidence that God knows where he is leading you?

Your hope should not be based on your understanding of God's purpose for you. Rather, your faith should be firmly grounded in God, who is bringing it about in you. Because even if that purpose seems very distant, you still trust him to successfully bring you to the destination.

> The LORD will fulfill his purpose for me; your love, O LORD, endures forever.
>
> PSALM 138:8 NIV

It is his able hand that works out his plans—not yours. Trust him to do exactly what is needed to bring them to fulfillment.

Dear God, I trust that you are a faithful and able leader. Thank you that my future is a work in your hands. Amen.

Many, O LORD my God, are the wonders you have done. The things you planned for us no one can recount to you; . . . they would be too many to declare.

PSALM 40:5 NIV

You Have Your Being

As you look into the mirror this morning, embrace this wonderful truth: God created everything about you. Your talents, personality, looks—the details that make you unique—were lovingly chosen by God.

This may cause you some astonishment if there are things about yourself that you don't like. However, you are precious to God. Everything he has given you—every facet of who you are—is lovely to him.

> **You are worthy, our Lord and God, to receive glory . . . for you created all things, and by your will they were created and have their being.**
> REVELATION 4:11 NIV

He built you with remarkable potential and has made no mistakes in constructing you. As you peer into the mirror, praise him for how he made you. He is truly a wonderful Creator.

Dear God, you really are worthy to receive glory. Thank you for loving me inside and out, and for how wonderfully you have created me. Amen.

You know me
inside and out,
you know every
bone in my
body; You know
exactly how I
was made, bit
by bit, how I
was sculpted
from nothing
into something.
PSALM 139:15 MSG

A Hearing Stance

This morning, before the daily commotion begins, find a place where you can be very quiet before God. Relinquish to God as an offering the things that fill your mind. Offer yourself as well, and listen.

Picture yourself before God's great throne. Imagine him in his holy temple. Is anything impossible for God?

> The Lord is in His holy temple; let all the earth hush and keep silence before Him.
>
> HABAKKUK 2:20 AMP

Let his Spirit speak deeply to your heart. What is he teaching you? Do you need forgiveness? Ask him. Does praise fill your heart? Sing.

Keep silent before him and fully enjoy the presence of the Lord God. Get yourself into a hearing stance, and he will surely give you the very words of life.

Dear God, I sit before you in quiet and joyful expectation. Truly, you are God. Show yourself in a mighty way through the stillness. Amen.

It is good that he waits silently
for the salvation of the Lord.

LAMENTATIONS 3:26 NASB

Of Your Word

You have heard the sales pitches, slick-talkers, and spin—the exaggerations and downright distortions of the truth. When looking for someone to trust, the search can get disheartening.

> **"Let your 'Yes' be 'Yes,' and your 'No,' 'No.'"**
> MATTHEW 5:37 NKJV

When Jesus taught the principle of yes and no, he was talking about being true to your word. When you mean yes, say yes without caveats or lengthy assertions—and then carry out whatever you have committed to do.

You will be a trustworthy person if you simply stand by your word and fulfill the promises you have made. People will believe what you say, not because of fancy words, but because they will know that you don't say it lightly.

Dear God, today help me to be straightforward in my responses and keep my promises so that I will be a trustworthy person. Amen.

You'll only hear true and right words from my mouth; not one syllable will be twisted or skewed.

PROVERBS 8:8 MSG

Get Unstuck and Believe

Have you ever been stuck between belief and unbelief?

It happens when there is no earthly solution to your dilemma and your only hope is that God will help you. Though you believe that God did miracles in ancient Israel, it is different trusting him to relieve your present-day problem. Can he *really* do it?

> I do believe; help
> my unbelief.
> MARK 9:24 NASB

Yet you are assured that anything is possible if you will just believe.

Just as he has worked powerfully throughout history, God is present and willing to work in your unique situation as well. Today, get unstuck by letting go of your doubts. Trust God to do the impossible for you, and truly believe.

Dear God, I do believe that you can do the impossible and that you will help me in my circumstances. Thank you. Amen.

**All things are possible
to him who believes.**

MARK 9:23 NKJV

Steadfast Trust

There is a confidence that goes beyond whatever has happened in the past or what may come to pass in the future. That confidence comes from trusting in God.

Thomas Manton wrote, "If a man would lead a happy life, let him but seek a sure object for his trust, and he shall be safe."

> **He will not fear bad news; his heart is confident, resting in the LORD.**
> PSALM 112:7 HCSB

Nothing in this world is certain, but the person who trusts in God is never disappointed. Every obstacle is an opportunity for God to show his power, every difficulty a way to learn from him and know his comfort.

Do not fear what is ahead. Instead, exercise your steadfast trust in God.

Dear God, even in this world of uncertainties, I will trust in you—the unfaltering and sure focus of my hope and affection. Amen.

Light arises in the darkness for the upright. . . . His heart is established and steady, he will not be afraid while he waits to see his desire established.

PSALM 112:4, 8 AMP

Strong in the Lord

God gives you spiritual armor to protect you as you live for him. It is all tied together with the belt of truth, which keeps you safely on the right path.

As you go, the breastplate of righteousness protects your heart from sin, and the helmet of salvation safeguards your mind with God's great promises. The shield of faith deflects the temptations that wound you, and the gospel gives you peace and purpose. Finally, the sword of the Spirit is your defensive weapon, your preparation for whatever comes.

> **Let the mighty strength of the Lord make you strong. Put on all the armor that God gives, so you can defend yourself.**
> Ephesians 6:10–11
> CEV

Today, put on God's armor and stand firm in him. Rejoice that you are clothed in his wonderful and mighty strength.

Dear God, thank you for clothing me in your spiritual armor. With you I will be strong. Amen.

The LORD loves what is right and does
not abandon his faithful people.
He protects them forever.

PSALM 37:28 GNT

Better Than Sacrifice

In the Old Testament, sacrifices were made to cover sins and maintain a right relationship with God. Yet sometimes people who participated in the rituals were not truly obedient or honest with God. Outwardly they did everything they were supposed to, but inwardly they were no different from those who disobeyed God outright.

> **To do righteousness and justice is more acceptable to the LORD than sacrifice.**
>
> PROVERBS 21:3 NKJV

The important thing to God is not that you go through the motions of religion but that you truly know him and love him more every day. Be honest with God today, and obey him. Your genuine change of heart will please him far more than any sacrifice you can dream up.

Dear God, thank you for caring about the condition of my heart even more than sacrifices. Help me always to do your will. Amen.

Loving him with all passion and intelligence and energy, and loving others as well as you love yourself. Why, that's better than all offerings and sacrifices put together!

MARK 12:33 MSG

Loving Living

You know you can't earn God's love, but how can you live your life in a manner that honors him and shows him you love him? The prophet Micah gives you some guidance.

First, *act justly*. Be a person of integrity and honesty, and love everyone impartially.

Second, *love mercy*. Always model God's compassion and grace to others.

Third, *walk humbly with your God*. Acknowledge that God's great wisdom is more than sufficient to guide you as you obey him.

This morning, your life will show how much you love God when you act justly, love mercy, and accept his instruction with humility.

> **What does the LORD require of you? To act justly and to love mercy and to walk humbly with your God.**
> MICAH 6:8 NIV

Dear God, help me to love you with my life and reflect your righteousness, compassion, and wisdom so that you will be glorified. Amen.

Love the LORD your God and
always obey all his laws.
DEUTERONOMY 11:1

Are You His?

How do you identify a Christian? Most people would describe a person who obeys a whole list of rules—including being a drug-free teetotaler who dislikes off-color jokes and only watches G-rated movies.

However, the most important defining factor for Christians is how they express their love.

> By this all people will know that you are My disciples, if you have love for one another.
> JOHN 13:35 HCSB

This is because when you love God, you obey him out of respect and caring—not out of ritual or fear. And when you love others, you humbly desire what is best for them—not analyze how they could benefit you.

Show that you are a Christian through your love for others today. People will surely know you are one of his.

Dear God, please increase my love for you and for others, so that people will know that I truly belong to you. Amen.

I give you a new commandment: love one another. Just as I have loved you, you must also love one another.

John 13:34 HCSB

Moments of Peace
for the Morning

**By this all people will know that
you are My disciples, if you have
love for one another.**

JOHN 13:35 HCSB

Winning With Praise

When Jehoshaphat was confronted with the armies of Ammon and Moab, he knew that his forces were no match for them. Yet he also knew that God had promised to help him. So as God instructed, Jehoshaphat gathered the people together to praise God.

> **Jehoshaphat appointed men to sing to the LORD and to praise him for the splendor of his holiness.**
> 2 CHRONICLES 20:21 NIV

You may think that this was a strange thing for Jehoshaphat to do. Yet God inhabits the praise of his people and gives them victory through it. With Jehoshaphat, God routed the enemy, and he never had to lift a sword.

He will help you too. Lift your voice in praise to him today, and watch as he helps you in a miraculous way.

Dear God, I praise the splendor of your holiness and the glory of your grace. Thank you for helping me in all my battles. Amen.

Jehoshaphat then led all the men of
Judah and Jerusalem back to Jerusalem—
an exuberant parade. God had given them
joyful relief from their enemies!

2 Chronicles 20:27 MSG

An Opportunity to Build

It had been fifty years since the temple had been destroyed. The Israelites longed to rebuild it, and when King Cyrus of Persia finally gave them the opportunity to do so, they were filled with great joy.

> **When the builders had finished laying the foundation of the temple, the priests put on their robes and blew trumpets in honor of the LORD.**
> EZRA 3:10 CEV

Any dream worth pursuing requires hard work—and sometimes just beginning the work takes a long time. Yet when you finally see God opening the door for you to pursue your aspirations, it will fill you with delight.

Are you waiting for your opportunity to build? Today take joy that you will soon see the foundation laid. God will be with you every step of the way.

Dear God, thank you for being the skilled architect of my dreams, and that my opportunity to build is just ahead. Amen.

They took turns singing: "The LORD is good! His faithful love for Israel will last forever." Everyone started shouting and praising the LORD because work on the foundation of the temple had begun.

EZRA 3:11 CEV

Anticipating a Glorious Future

This is a promise for you to claim today. Your pressures and trials—however difficult they may be—will be like nothing to you when God's glory is revealed.

Hurts, stresses, and frustrations—they all belong to this world. God uses them for good to teach you character, patience, humility, and faith.

> I consider that the sufferings of this present time are not worth comparing with the glory that is to be revealed to us.
> ROMANS 8:18 ESV

Yet the glory belongs solely to God. It is the achievement of his good plan and the splendor of his presence, and he freely shares both with you.

Claim this promise today, and look forward to the great things God will reveal to you. Anticipate the fabulously glorious future.

Dear God, I can endure my present problems because I know that your plan will be fulfilled and that I will see your wonderful glory. Amen.

If we are God's children, we will receive blessings from God together with Christ. But we must suffer as Christ suffered so that we will have glory as Christ has glory.

ROMANS 8:17 NCV

Seeing His Face

This benediction that God gave as a blessing to the Israelites is given to you this morning. May God bless your day by showing himself to you and giving you a peaceful heart.

His mercy and compassion are cause for praise. His approval and blessing are like a nourishing spring filling you with joy. Though he rules all of heaven and earth, he cares for you, knows your deepest hopes, and gives you tranquility in the midst of the storms.

> The LORD look with favor on you and give you peace.
>
> NUMBERS 6:26 HCSB

This is the heart of your God—shining his light on your life and being gracious to you. So turn your face toward him this morning and praise him.

Dear God, thank you for showing me your beautiful face. I praise you for your peace and goodness—for your comfort, wisdom, grace, and protection. Amen.

The Lord bless you and watch, guard, and keep you; the Lord make His face to shine upon and enlighten you and be gracious (kind, merciful, and giving favor) to you.

NUMBERS 6:24–25 AMP

Nothing at All

The situation looked desperate. The Babylonians were poised for attack and the people of Judah refused to ask God for help. The prophet Jeremiah knew that if the Babylonians carried off all the people, as was their practice, the Promised Land would be lost to God's people for good. God assured Jeremiah that the land was safe because it was in his hands.

> I am the LORD, the God of all the peoples of the world. Is anything too hard for me?
>
> JEREMIAH 32:27 NLT

Impossible situations are God's specialty. At times, it will seem that if anything can go wrong, it does. But nothing is too difficult for God. You can have patience during times of difficulty knowing that all the obstacles in your path are nothing at all to God.

Dear God, thank you that impossible situations are your specialty and that nothing is too hard for you. I count on your wonderful might. Amen.

Ah Lord GOD! Behold, You have made the heavens and the earth by Your great power and by Your outstretched arm! Nothing is too difficult for You.

JEREMIAH 32:17 NASB

Absolutely Possible

It was truly shocking to discover that elderly, barren Elizabeth was pregnant. Yet when young Mary went to visit her, she had even more miraculous news. Mary, a virgin, was going to have a baby too.

> **Nothing is impossible for God!**
> LUKE 1:37 CEV

Some miracles are not only incredible; they are downright beyond belief, almost. Your most wonderful promises from God may seem like utter foolishness to others—not just improbable, but patently impossible. In fact, if it were not for your faith, you wouldn't believe them either.

Don't worry—you are not peculiar. God often does the impossible to show his glory. And just as a virgin can have a baby, God can bring whatever he promised you into being too.

Dear God, I thank you that even inconceivable things are absolutely possible with you. Thank you for doing the impossible for me. Amen.

**The Mighty One has done
great things for me, and
His name is holy.**

LUKE 1:49 HCSB

He Knows the Way

"What is God's will for me?" Everyone asks that question at one point or another, especially during decision-making times. People try to be very conscious of God's will because they fear disappointing him and missing his blessings.

> **Whether you turn to the right or to the left, your ears will hear a voice behind you, saying, "This is the way; walk in it."**
>
> ISAIAH 30:21 NIV

God's will is for you to be so close to him that you are confident that he is always leading you. True, the way may sometimes seem confusing or obscure. But God knows the way—the best way—to take you.

Today, listen to God, and he will make his will known to you. Then obey him as he reveals the path. You may find that you are already walking in it.

Dear God, thank you for teaching me your will. Help me to be so close to you that I always know I am doing what you want. Amen.

I guide you in the way of wisdom and lead you along straight paths. When you walk, your steps will not be hampered; when you run, you will not stumble.

Proverbs 4:11–12 NIV

More Power Than That?

Think about the power that God exerted when Christ was resurrected. That power took on the sin of the world and destroyed it. It took the shackles from death and demolished them. And it forever changed how humanity relates to God.

No small power was exerted there. In fact, the imagination can barely conceive it. Yet it is the same power that has been given to help you in your every need.

> **Understand the incredible greatness of his power for us who believe him. This is the same mighty power that raised Christ from the dead.**
> EPHESIANS 1:19–20
> NLT

You have not been left alone to fend for yourself. God has given you his great power. Rejoice today that you will never have a problem that requires more power than that.

Dear God, I cannot think of a situation that needs more power than the resurrection. Thank you for making that power available to me. Amen.

God, You are awe-inspiring in Your sanctuaries. The God of Israel gives power and strength to His people. May God be praised!

Empowering for Good

The desire you have to serve God comes from him. Whether it is because of thankfulness for your salvation, out of a desire for others to know him, or through his call for you to live for him—all of those feelings are evidence of God working in you.

> **God is working in you, giving you the desire to obey him and the power to do what pleases him.**
> PHILIPPIANS 2:13 NLT

Do not be afraid about how you will serve. Do not question whether you are strong, good-looking, smart, or talented enough to do a good job for him. And do not fret over your faults or weaknesses. He will provide you with everything you need, and he will accomplish amazingly good things through you.

Dear God, thank you for my desire to serve you. I praise you for giving me the power to do whatever you call me to. Amen.

May our Lord Jesus
Christ Himself and
God our Father, who
has loved us and
given us eternal com-
fort and good hope
by grace, comfort
and strengthen your
hearts in every good
work and word.

2 THESSALONIANS 2:16–17
NASB

An Intermission to Your Dreams

When Joseph was young, God gave him the dream of being a great leader. Yet many difficult things happened that seemed to completely contradict that vision. Undoubtedly, Joseph must have wondered if what he had dreamed was a mistake.

> **God has prospered me in the land of my sorrow.**
> GENESIS 41:52 MSG

Thankfully, God used those hard things in Joseph's life to prepare him to be Pharaoh's top advisor.

You also will have experiences that seemingly distance you from your dreams. However, if you stick close to God, he will give you success.

Today, take heart that your experiences are not a change of course. Rather, they are simply an intermission to the great dreams God is making real in you.

Dear God, I praise you for working powerfully in the intermissions. Thank you for making the dream real in me. Amen.

The LORD was with him.
And whatever he did,
the LORD made it succeed.
GENESIS 39:23 ESV

He Cares for You

You can let go of your fears. In fact, it is imperative that you do because your worries impede you from enjoying the life God has given you.

Today, cast all of your cares—the anxieties, doubts, and all of the things that distract, irritate, and drive you crazy—upon him. For once and for all, give each one—from the least to the greatest—to God so that he can carry them for you.

> **Give all your worries and cares to God, for he cares about what happens to you.**
> 1 PETER 5:7 NLT

Allow him to care for you—everything that concerns or has an effect on you. He loves you greatly, and he will faithfully handle everything better than you could ever hope to. Praise his holy name.

Dear God, it is hard to let go of my fears. Yet I give them to you and trust you to care for me. Amen.

Give your worries to the Lord, and he will take care of you. He will never let good people down.

Psalm 55:22 NCV

Finding Mercy

The truth about sin is that you do more harm to yourself when you hide it than when you confess it openly to God. This is because when you conceal it, it creates a destructive cycle within you.

> **Whoever conceals his transgressions will not prosper, but he who confesses and forsakes them will obtain mercy.**
> PROVERBS 28:13 ESV

Yet when you confess it, you acknowledge you need God's mercy and strength to help you. God sets you free from the damaging cycle by working on its root cause—removing the fear, bitterness, and corruption that spawned it.

God heals you, loves you, and gives your life significance and success. Confess your sins to him today so that he can teach you real freedom and you can find mercy.

Dear God, I do confess my sin to you. Thank you for your great mercy and for giving me such wonderful freedom. Amen.

Count yourself lucky, how happy you must be—you get a fresh start, your slate's wiped clean. Count yourself lucky—GOD holds nothing against you and you're holding nothing back from him.

PSALM 32:1–2 MSG

The Blessed Believe to See

Very few had Thomas's opportunity—seeing and touching Jesus on earth after his resurrection. Jesus said you would be especially blessed because you have not seen him, and yet you believe.

This is the essence of faith—not seeing, but always trusting. Jesus overcame sin and gave you a new life. It is not a truth that you can grasp with your hands as Thomas did. You must believe in order to see God. You must have confidence before God can bless your life.

> **Have you believed because you have seen me? Blessed are those who have not seen and yet have believed.**
> JOHN 20:29 ESV

Today, forget your doubts. Believe God and be blessed by how clearly he shows himself to you.

Dear God, I do believe you, and I thank you that one day I will see your face. Amen.

These are written that you may believe that
Jesus is the Christ, the Son of God, and that
believing you may have life in His name.

JOHN 20:31 NKJV

Remember

This morning, take a moment to remember the wonderful deeds of God. Remember how he showed his mighty power in the Bible and in the lives of the people you love.

Remember how God has revealed himself to you and has worked in your life. Remember how he acted in the past on your behalf and how he orchestrated circumstances just to show you how deeply and intimately he cares about you. Remember the times the Bible gave you peace and God's presence gave you joy.

> I remember your wonderful deeds of long ago. They are constantly in my thoughts. I cannot stop thinking about them.
> PSALM 77:11–12 NLT

Remember all these things today so that you can remain faithful to him and so that your hope will remain strong.

Dear God, fill my thoughts with your wonderful deeds and remind me of your works, and I will sing your praise all day long. Amen.

O God, your ways are holy. Is there any god as mighty as you? You are the God of miracles and wonders! You demonstrate your awesome power among the nations.

PSALM 77:13–14 NLT

Moments of Peace for the Morning

Give all your worries and
cares to God, for he cares
about what happens to you.

1 PETER 5:7 NLT

A Way Out

You will have temptations today—that is a basic truth of the Christian life. However, just because you have temptations does not mean you will necessarily sin. Just the opposite. Because you have temptations, you have a unique opportunity for success.

> **When you are tempted, he will show you a way out so that you will not give in to it.**
>
> 1 Corinthians 10:13
> NLT

The word that Paul used here for *tempted* is also translated as *tested*. These tests can make you stronger if you seek God in them and take the way out he gives you.

This morning, set your heart on God and resolve that you will listen to him when temptation comes your way. He will show you an excellent way out—a way that leads you to victory.

Dear God, thank you for giving me a way of escape from my temptations. Help me always to grow stronger through the tests. Amen.

The Lord knows how to
rescue the godly from
temptation.

2 PETER 2:9 NASB

Slow to React

Here is a picture of God that should be imitated by believers—he is compassionate, gracious, slow to anger, and abundant in faithful love and truth.

How very different from what is recommended by worldly sources. Society suggests that in order to achieve, one must be ruthless—quick to react and make decisions.

> You, Lord, are a compassionate and gracious God, slow to anger and abundant in faithful love and truth.
>
> PSALM 86:15 HCSB

Yet this is God's will—that you not *react* but that you set yourself to be *proactive*.

Be like God in your attitude toward others—not making quick judgments, but slowly and deliberately acting with tenderness and self-control. By doing so, you bring honor to God, build up the people around you, and keep conflict from building.

Dear God, please help me to slow down when reacting to others so that I may treat them with compassion, love, and truth. Amen.

People who make fun of wisdom cause trouble in a city, but wise people calm anger down.

PROVERBS 29:8 NCV

Unconditional

King David wanted to honor his best friend Jonathan, who was killed in battle. He sought out Jonathan's children in order to show them kindness on Jonathan's behalf. The only one living was Mephibosheth—a sad, crippled man.

Fearfully, Mephibosheth expressed his unworthiness before the king. Why would David bother with him? David welcomed him wholeheartedly into his home because of his great love for Jonathan.

> **Mephibosheth knelt down again and said, "Why should you care about me?"**
> 2 Samuel 9:8 CEV

Any fears you have regarding God are similarly unfounded. When God looks at you, he sees Jesus in you and responds in love.

Today, enter God's presence with confidence and experience his unconditional love.

Dear God, thank you for loving me unconditionally and welcoming me wholeheartedly. Your love is too wonderful for words. Amen.

May your unfailing love rest upon us,
O Lord, even as we put our hope in you.
Psalm 33:22 niv

An Attitude of Love

Novelist and minister Ian Maclaren wrote, "Be kind, everyone you meet is carrying a heavy burden." This is why Jesus treated everyone with such wonderful compassion. He knew that every person deals with difficult things that influence how they react. He also knew that people didn't need more burdens—they needed more love. And so he cared for everyone, regardless of how they responded to him.

> **Christ sacrificed his life for us. This is why we ought to live sacrificially for our fellow believers.**
> 1 JOHN 3:16 MSG

As you meet people today, take this truth to heart and have an attitude of love. Though you cannot see why people react the way they do, you can be a blessing to them. Even if they cannot reciprocate, they will surely see God in you.

Dear God, thank you for knowing the burdens I bear. Help me to love other people as you do. Amen.

I led them with
cords of human
kindness, with ties of
love; I lifted the
yoke from their neck
and bent down to
feed them.

HOSEA 11:4 NIV

A Hopeful Expectancy

Changed from an arid, barren land to a plush paradise. Transformed from a stony terrain to a flourishing botanical wonderland. This is the inheritance of those who believe in God.

> **The LORD will surely comfort Zion . . . he will make her deserts like Eden, her wastelands like the garden of the LORD.**
>
> ISAIAH 51:3 NIV

Every believer goes through periods of dryness in his or her spiritual life—times of confusion when it is difficult to hear God or perceive that he is still leading. You may even feel that you have stopped growing spiritually.

These times should not wither your trust in him. Rather, they should nourish your hopeful expectancy in the hearty fruitfulness to come. For God will surely comfort you and turn all your deserts into havens of beauty and grace.

Dear God, thank you for comforting me during these dry, confusing times. I praise you that soon I will see renewal and fruitfulness. Amen.

Those who have been ransomed by the LORD will return to Jerusalem, singing songs of everlasting joy. Sorrow and mourning will disappear, and they will be overcome with joy and gladness.

ISAIAH 51:11 NLT

Giving Thanks for You

Thankful—that is to be your attitude toward others. Believers are challenged to look at their loved ones, friends, co-workers, neighbors, and acquaintances with a spirit of gratefulness.

> **I never stop giving thanks for you as I remember you in my prayers.**
> EPHESIANS 1:16 HCSB

Know that as you read this meditation this morning, someone is giving thanks for you—for God's work in your life and for what you mean to the people around you. You are also called to give thanks for those you know. Even if those people are difficult, you can praise God that he is teaching you through them.

You will be amazed at how much God will bless you—making your love for them and for him grow through your thankfulness.

Dear God, I am thankful for the people around me. Thank you for growing me through them and increasing my love for them. Amen.

Every time I think of you—
and I think of you often!—
I thank God for your lives
of free and open access to
God, given by Jesus.

1 CORINTHIANS 1:4 MSG

On Your Side

The king of Aram was angry because the prophet Elisha kept foiling his plans. He sent his forces to capture Elisha.

When Elisha's servant saw what was happening, he was thoroughly frightened. Elisha prayed that the servant's eyes would be opened to what was happening spiritually so that he could see that they were not alone. God's mighty forces protected them.

> **Don't be afraid, for those who are with us outnumber those who are with them.**
> 2 KINGS 6:16 HCSB

Today you may feel like Elisha's servant—overwhelmed with the problems that confront you. However, God is on your side, and his powerful resources are encamped around you. Ask him to open your eyes so that you may behold the mighty power he has prepared for your defense.

Dear God, help me to see your active defense on my behalf. Thank you for being on my side. I never need to fear. Amen.

Defend my cause, and set me free;
save me, as you have promised.

PSALM 119:154 GNT

Seek and Pursue

It is the image of a runner eagerly and steadfastly racing toward the finish line. This is how the apostle Peter described the important pursuit of peace. Peace cannot be achieved passively. Rather, it is an aspiration you must strive for and be proactive about.

> **Seek peace and pursue it.**
> 1 PETER 3:11 NKJV

First, you must care about others and be earnestly concerned about their well-being. Then you must do your best not to create or give in to conflicts—as long as they do not compromise your core values. Finally, when conflicts do arise, you must deal with them swiftly and constructively.

Invest yourself in the pursuit of peace. You will be greatly pleased at the returns you receive.

Dear God, peace is a difficult thing to achieve, but I set myself to pursue it—to your honor and glory. Amen.

Agree and have concern and love for each other. You should also be kind and humble. Don't be hateful and insult people. . . . Treat everyone with kindness. You are God's chosen ones, and he will bless you.

1 PETER 3:8–9 CEV

To Soar as Eagles

They say that eagles in flight take no concern for obstacles below. How wonderful it would be to forget all earthly constraints and challenges and soar high above—carried effortlessly by air currents and refreshing breezes.

There are mornings when you will wake up tired. You will feel how truly earthbound you are and come to the conclusion that your gravity-defying goals are too lofty to hope for.

> **They shall lift their wings and mount up [close to God] as eagles [mount up to the sun].**
>
> ISAIAH 40:31 AMP

Take heart today that God never grows tired or weary. He promises to renew your strength when you wait upon him. And like the powerful, majestic eagle, he will lift you high above the obstacles of earth—and you will soar.

Dear God, thank you for helping me to soar like an eagle. I will not think of the obstacles but will praise your wonderful strength. Amen.

The LORD . . . does not become tired or need to rest. No one can understand how great his wisdom is. He gives strength to those who are tired and more power to those who are weak.

ISAIAH 40:28–29 NCV

Lord, I Know You Will

God is waiting for you to get quiet before him—to cast aside your worries and truly seek the tranquility of his presence. He is God—the almighty and wonderful, your powerful defender and loving friend. He is the Lord who makes you whole and gives you the desires of your heart.

> **Be still in the presence of the LORD, and wait patiently for him to act.**
> PSALM 37:7 NLT

He is waiting for your heart to be calm—for you to realize that nothing in heaven or on earth can stop him from doing good things on your behalf. He is waiting for you—by your silence and quiet trust—to express your confidence that he will do as he promised.

Today, be still before him. And know him.

Dear God, silence is a challenge. Help my spirit to be calm and quiet before you so that I may know you and trust you more. Amen.

Don't be impatient for the LORD to act!
Travel steadily along his path. He will
honor you, giving you the land.
PSALM 37:34 NLT

Before and Behind

There are two intrinsic factors that will shape how you carry out your day today—the past and the future. Your history will influence your attitudes and beliefs, reactions and fears. Your future will be instrumental in how you plan and will be based upon your goals and hopes.

> **The LORD will go before you, and the God of Israel will be your rear guard.**
> ISAIAH 52:12 ESV

God is fully with you today and always—timelessly guarding and guiding your path. He brings good out of the experiences in your yesterdays that have shaped you, and prepares you for what will happen in your tomorrows.

God goes behind you, protecting you, and before you, pointing you in the right direction. Rejoice that as you follow him, he fully safeguards your days.

Dear God, thank you for being with me in my yesterdays and in my tomorrows. I praise you for blessing all the days of my life. Amen.

May the LORD bless you from Zion, so that you will see the prosperity of Jerusalem all the days of your life.

PSALM 128:5 HCSB

An Easy Yoke

Your relationship with God is not meant to enslave you but to set you free. The yoke, which was used for plowing, was useless if it was too heavy. Yet a good yoke harnessed the power of the oxen in order to accomplish more.

> **Take My yoke upon you and learn from Me, for I am gentle and lowly in heart, and you will find rest for your souls.**
> MATTHEW 11:29 NKJV

That is why God does not burden you or wear you out with a strict religious regimen. Rather, he offers you a life-giving relationship so that together with him you can accomplish more.

This morning, God offers you his sweet assurance that he will give you rest for your soul. So go to him, learn from him, and find the yoke that fits best of all.

Dear God, thank you for removing the burden of religion and for giving me rest. I am honored to be yoked together with you. Amen.

Are you tired? Worn out? Burned out on religion? Come to me. Get away with me and you'll recover your life. I'll show you how to take a real rest.

MATTHEW 11:28 MSG

Even Greater

Are you humbled by the thought that you could do greater things than Jesus? What could be greater than being raised from the dead and providing eternal life for all of humanity?

> **If you have faith in me, you will do the same things that I am doing. You will do even greater things.**
> JOHN 14:12 CEV

Yet the meaning here is not about bigger miracles—it is about honoring God. Jesus' purpose was to provide the way to God so that others could know him. Now that he has provided the way, you can know God, and he can shine through you.

Jesus saw the potential you have to bring glory to God. Today, emulate his example by telling others of how great a gift it is to honor him with your life.

Dear God, thank you for the great purpose of introducing others to you. I am honored to live for you and to give you all the glory. Amen.

When you become fruitful
disciples of mine, my Father
will be honored.

JOHN 15:8 CEV

Unfailing Compassion

You are not done—your hope has not come to an end. That is what Jeremiah meant when he wrote that because of God's love you would not perish.

> [Because of] the LORD's faithful love we do not perish, for His mercies never end.
>
> LAMENTATIONS 3:22
> HCSB

Because God's goodness, kindness, and faithfulness have no end, you can eagerly expect that he again will make all things bright and hopeful. Just as his mercy is renewed every morning, so also can your dreams have innumerable new beginnings.

Give thanks to God for his unfailing compassion that gives you a fresh start this morning. Whatever happened yesterday is washed clean and transformed by God's abundant love for you. Today you will experience how truly great his faithfulness is.

Dear God, I do thank you for your wonderful, unfailing compassion. Thank you for bringing new beginnings to all of my dreams. Amen.

Deep in my heart I say, "The Lord is all I need; I can depend on him!" The Lord is kind to everyone who trusts and obeys him.

LAMENTATIONS 3:24–25 CEV

Moments of Peace for the Morning

May the words of my mouth and the thoughts of my heart be pleasing to you, O LORD, my rock and my redeemer.

PSALM 19:14 NLT

What Counts

Who would be Israel's new king? Samuel knew it was to be one of Jesse's sons. But which one? As the men filed past him, God told Samuel to keep looking.

Finally, Jesse's youngest son, David, came in from tending sheep, and God directed Samuel to set him apart as king. Though he was handsome and brave, God's reason for choosing David was his heart—the love David had for God and his great faith.

> The LORD does not see as man sees; for man looks at the outward appearance, but the LORD looks at the heart.
>
> 1 SAMUEL 16:7 NKJV

That is what counts for you as well. God chooses you—not because of your looks or strength, but because you love God and are willing to serve him faithfully.

Dear God, thank you that what matters most to you is my heart. Help me to love you more so that I may please you. Amen.

Serve Him with a whole heart and a willing mind, for the LORD searches every heart and understands the intention of every thought. If you seek Him, He will be found by you.

1 CHRONICLES 28:9 HCSB

He Will Remember

The Israelites stood on the brink of claiming the Promised Land. God encouraged them by vowing to remember his covenant. The challenge of conquering the land was intimidating, and yet they knew that with God empowering them, they would succeed.

> The LORD your God will have mercy—he won't destroy you or desert you. The LORD will remember his promise.
> DEUTERONOMY 4:31
> CEV

As you come to the edge of the promise God has given to you, you may be overwhelmed with the work ahead or the things that remain unknown. But God brought you to this point, and he will not forget what he promised you. You will succeed.

Today, praise him that he remembers the promise and will be with you every step of the way to achieving it.

Dear God, this is intimidating, and I thank you for remembering your promise to me. I know that with your help, I will succeed. Amen.

He has made His wonders to be remembered; the LORD is gracious and compassionate. . . . He will remember His covenant forever. He has made known to His people the power of His works.

PSALM 111:4–6 NASB

From Few to Many

What are your talents? What gifts do you possess? Everyone has things that they do well. That includes you. You have many special abilities that you could use to glorify God.

The interesting thing about your gift is that as you use them, you gain more. That is because God rewards faithfulness. When he sees that you are a good manager of what he has given to you, he expands your abilities and your opportunities for success.

> You were faithful with a few things, I will put you in charge of many things; enter into the joy of your master.
>
> MATTHEW 25:21 NASB

Today, make a list of what you do well and pray about how God wants you to serve him. He will find you faithful, and you will share his joy.

Dear God, I want to be faithful and honor you with my abilities. Please show me how you would like for me to serve you. Amen.

To those who use well what they are given, even more will be given, and they will have an abundance.

MATTHEW 25:29 NLT

Seeing to Believe?

Thomas's sorrow was so great that he could not believe what the other disciples were saying. After all, he had seen Jesus on the cross. With his own eyes he watched Jesus breathe his last breath. How could the others say he was raised from the grave?

> **Take your finger and examine my hands. . . . Don't be unbelieving. Believe.**
> JOHN 20:27 MSG

God understands that at times it is difficult for your heart to recover from what your eyes have seen. Yet he still calls you to believe.

This message is especially for you this morning, because your heart needs to take hold of what has been hidden from your eyes. Believe God and rejoice that his power goes beyond anything that you've ever seen.

Dear God, I do believe, even though I cannot see. Thank you for working in the unseen and always giving me hope. Amen.

Through Christ you have come to trust in God. And because God raised Christ from the dead and gave him great glory, your faith and hope can be placed confidently in God.

1 PETER 1:21 NLT

Because He Is

Hippocrates said, "Things that are holy are revealed only to men who are holy." True, God himself made you holy through Jesus. Yet your forgiven inward condition should be demonstrated through your outward activities. And the more you imitate God's holiness, the better you will know him.

> I am the Lord your God; so consecrate yourselves and be holy, for I am holy.
>
> LEVITICUS 11:44 AMP

The word *holy* means "to be set apart." You have been set apart for God—to both imitate and represent him. As you faithfully do so, he is able to teach you more deeply, empower you more mightily, and shine through you more brightly.

Be holy today because he is, and he will reveal himself in a more profound way than ever before.

Dear God, I do want to know you more and be holy because you are holy. Thank you for revealing yourself to me. Amen.

To the one who comes near me,
I will show myself holy; before all
the people, I will show my glory.

LEVITICUS 10:3 MSG

Lawful Versus Helpful

How do you balance the freedom you have in Christ and the proper conduct for a Christian? Aren't Christians able to live as they please—knowing they've been set free from the sinful nature?

> **All things are lawful for me, but all things are not helpful.**
>
> 1 CORINTHIANS 6:12
> NKJV

Though it is true that God has forgiven you of your sins and that sin no longer has power over you, you should still avoid it. This is for the simple reason that certain actions not only hinder your growing relationship with God but may also impede others from seeking him.

Those actions may be lawful for you, but they aren't helpful to anyone. Today, practice only those activities that are helpful to your growing relationship with God.

Dear God, I want to live a life that is worthy of you. Please help me to choose only those activities that honor you. Amen.

People should think of us as servants of Christ, the ones God has trusted with his secrets. Now in this way those who are trusted with something valuable must show they are worthy of that trust.

1 CORINTHIANS 4:1–2
NCV

Show Me, Lord

In every relationship, there is a certain amount of guesswork involved when pleasing the other person. You never completely know how to best satisfy his or her expectations.

This is not so with God. You never have to guess what is pleasing to God because he communicates his desires to your innermost being. His Spirit either confirms you are on the right path or shows you how you have strayed.

> May the words of my mouth and the thoughts of my heart be pleasing to you, O LORD, my rock and my redeemer.
>
> PSALM 19:14 NLT

The God who saves you is also able to teach you how to live in a manner that is pleasing to him. Even now he is speaking to your Spirit and giving you the ability to do as he asks.

Dear God, thank you for teaching me what you want, and for giving me the ability to do it. May my life always please you. Amen.

Teach me to do Your will, for You are my God; let Your good Spirit lead me on level ground.

PSALM 143:10 NASB

Your Best

Love bears all things. As Jesus faithfully bears your weaknesses, so faithfully bear his strength in helping others.

Believes all things. As Jesus believes your life is worth sacrificing his, so believe that proclaiming his good news of salvation is worth investing yours.

> **Love bears all things, believes all things, hopes all things, endures all things.**
>
> 1 CORINTHIANS 13:7
> ESV

Hopes all thing. As Jesus hopes that you will willingly reflect his image, so maintain the hope that anything that comes into your life works toward that end.

Endures all things. As Jesus endured the cross to provide you eternal life, so obediently endure this life in order to give him glory.

Just as Jesus has given you his best, so freely give him yours.

Dear God, I know your love never fails. Help me to give my best by bearing, believing, hoping, and enduring all things in your love. Amen.

Let whoever is wise pay attention
to these things and consider the
LORD's acts of faithful love.

PSALM 107:43 HCSB

Seeing Your Joy Complete

When the wall of Jerusalem had been rebuilt, the Israelites did not congratulate themselves for fortifying the city. Though they all had worked very hard and had sacrificed a great deal, they realized that they had only played a small part. Their accomplishment would never have been possible apart from God's help and provision.

> On that day they offered great sacrifices and rejoiced because God had given them great joy.
>
> NEHEMIAH 12:43 HCSB

Imitate their example today and praise God for the victories and achievements he has helped you to attain. God empowered you and paved the way for success.

You will find that your joy is more abundant and complete when you acknowledge the God who loved you and helped you bring your accomplishments into being.

Dear God, thank you so much for making my goals realities. It is because of you that I have success, and I praise your wonderful name. Amen.

Our God didn't abandon us. He has put us in the good graces of the kings of Persia and given us the heart to build The Temple of our God, restore its ruins, and construct a defensive wall in Judah and Jerusalem.

EZRA 9:9 MSG

A Merry Face

When you are a person of praise, everyone knows it. It shows in your words and actions. It even shows in your countenance.

Praise expresses your confidence that God is with you—no matter what comes. It helps you remember the faithful love of God that sustains you and the profound wisdom of God that guides you. And it changes your focus from your limited understanding to the wonderful strength and power of God.

> A twinkle in the eye means joy in the heart, and good news makes you feel fit as a fiddle.
> PROVERBS 15:30 MSG

God becomes the light of your eyes and the good news of your heart. Praise God today, and people will know by your merry face that you have been in his presence.

Dear God, the thought of you puts a smile on my face. I praise you for your goodness and might—your love, wisdom, and power. Amen.

It is good to praise you, LORD. . . . It is good to tell of your love in the morning and of your loyalty at night. . . . LORD, you have made me happy by what you have done.

PSALM 92:1–2, 4 NCV

Security in His Word

The centurion knew that Jesus was true to his word. That is why he did not ask Jesus to go all the way to his house when his servant was sick. If Jesus said so, the servant would be healed. And sure enough, the servant was well from that very moment.

Does that rule hold for you? When God speaks to you through prayer or the Bible, do you take him at his word?

You have security in the Bible—it is absolutely true—and what God says will certainly be accomplished. Today, believe wholeheartedly so that, like the centurion, you will be commended for your faith.

> Say the word, and my servant will be healed.
>
> LUKE 7:7 NKJV

Dear God, the Bible is wonderful, and I believe it is true. Help me to cling to the certainty of the Bible. Amen.

When Jesus heard this, he was amazed. Turning to the crowd that was following him, he said, "I tell you, this is the greatest faith I have found anywhere."

LUKE 7:9 NCV

Moments of Peace
for the Morning

My God will supply all your
needs according to His riches
in glory in Christ Jesus.

PHILIPPIANS 4:19 HCSB

Making Peace

There may be people in your life that—no matter how accommodating and nice you are—will not return your friendship. It can be frustrating. You want to have peace, but they prefer conflict.

If you respond in anger, there will never be harmony between you. However, when you continue to treat them with kindness, eventually you prevail over whatever feelings they have against you. You don't have to surrender your principles—you must simply assert them with gentleness and wisdom.

> **Do your best to live at peace with everyone.**
> ROMANS 12:18 CEV

The only way to sway your rivals is to pray for them and be kind. You will find that as you were busy making peace, you were also making a friend.

Dear God, please show me how to be kind to those who are abrasive. Thank you for helping me overcome their evil with good. Amen.

Do what the Scriptures say: "If your enemies are hungry, feed them . . . and they will be ashamed of what they have done to you." Don't let evil get the best of you, but conquer evil by doing good.

ROMANS 12:20–21 NLT

Big Obstacles

The people were like giants—or so reported ten of the spies who scoped out the land promised to them by God. Though they were so very close to receiving the desire of their hearts—a land of their own—they were so intimidated by the obstacles that they wanted to give up.

> [Caleb said,] "Let's go and take the land. I know we can do it!"
> NUMBERS 13:30 CEV

However, Joshua and Caleb knew that with God's help, no obstacle could stop them. Take this to heart today: No obstacle is too big for you when God is with you. Obstacles are object lessons for your faith—they cannot prevent what God has promised you.

Go today and claim the land that God has promised you. You can do it.

Dear God, with your help, I can do it. I thank you, my God, that no obstacle is ever too big for you to fulfill your promises. Amen.

Do not be afraid of the people of the land, because we will swallow them up. Their protection is gone, but the LORD is with us. Do not be afraid of them.

NUMBERS 14:9 NIV

Believe God

Your life and how you conduct yourself both hinge on whether or not you believe God. Take Abraham, for example. He willingly did all God asked him to do because he wholeheartedly trusted God. And God called him a friend.

> **The Scripture was fulfilled which says, "Abraham believed God, and it was accounted to him for right-eousness." And he was called the friend of God.**
> JAMES 2:23 NKJV

That is why people are still encouraged by Abraham's story today—because of his great faith and how God blessed him and the world through it.

Every day you have the same choice as Abraham—believe God and do as he says or not. You can make an extraordinary difference in the world if you will step out in faith. Will you believe God and be his friend?

Dear God, I want to have great faith and be your friend. I'll follow you, believing that you know the best path for my life. Amen.

Abraham's faith and
deeds worked
together. He proved
that his faith was
real by what he did.
JAMES 2:22 CEV

Glorious Provision

Paul had experienced it—God's glorious provision. He had seen God's help in a powerful way through the very church in Philippi to which he lovingly penned this letter. They had been very generous with him, and he assured the church that God was going to bless them because of it.

> My God will supply all your needs according to His riches in glory in Christ Jesus.
> PHILIPPIANS 4:19 HCSB

This is a wonderful promise for you to claim today. As you are generous with others, you never have to fear being short in resources for your own needs. On the contrary—you open yourself up to God's glorious supply.

Rejoice and freely share with others today. You will certainly receive the great provision God has reserved just for you.

Dear God, thank you that as I give to others I don't need to fear for my own needs. I praise you for your wonderful provision. Amen.

You are rich in everything—in faith, in speaking, in knowledge, in truly wanting to help, and in the love you learned from us. In the same way, be strong also in the grace of giving.

2 CORINTHIANS 8:7 NCV

Seasons of Blessings

Throughout Israel's history, the success or failure of Israel hinged on two short rainy seasons. Everything depended on the precipitation. If it rained well, there would be plenty of crops. If it did not, there would be famine and devastation.

It was easy for them to look at the cloudless sky and fear that the dry days would continue. Perhaps this morning it is the same in your life. It feels like nothing is going to change—that the rains of abundance will not pour forth for you.

> **He did good by giving you rains from heaven and fruitful seasons, satisfying your hearts with food and gladness.**
> ACTS 14:17 ESV

Just as God faithfully sent the rain for fruitful seasons, trust him to send you showers of blessings that will satisfy you and gladden your heart.

Dear God, thank you for sending your showers of blessings at just the right time. You are truly good to me. Amen.

The LORD will open up his heavenly
storehouse so that the skies send rain
on your land at the right time, and he
will bless everything you do.
DEUTERONOMY 28:12 NCV

His Work Is Wonderful

You are God's special creation. When he formed you, he was delighted to give you all the qualities that make you unique—your traits and talents. Yet even the things you consider flaws and weaknesses were all part of his perfecting you—his wonderful one.

> **You knitted me together in my mother's womb. I praise you, for I am fearfully and wonderfully made.**
>
> PSALM 139:13–14
> ESV

He made no mistakes in constructing you. In fact, those aspects you feel are errors are actually his mark on your life—what he used in a powerful way to make himself known to you.

This morning, rejoice that you have been excellently formed by your wonderful maker, and fulfill that precious part of his great plan that has been specially created for you.

Dear God, thank you for creating me the way I am. I praise you that all of your works are truly wonderful. Amen.

With your own eyes
you saw my body being
formed. Even before I
was born, you had
written in your book
everything I would do.
PSALM 139:16 CEV

With You to the End

This was the comforting promise Jesus gave to the disciples when he sent them out to tell the good news of salvation. Through the Holy Spirit, Jesus would help them wherever they went.

> **I'll be with you as you do this, day after day after day, right up to the end of the age.**
> MATTHEW 28:20 MSG

This is God's promise to you as well. He knows that life can get lonely—especially when you deal with personal issues that are difficult to share with others. Yet you are never alone. God is right there for you—always caring for the deep issues of your heart.

This morning, pray to your constant friend and allow him to fill you with his comfort. He loves you and is with you to the end.

Dear God, thank you for being with me in the issues I can't share with others. Thank you for never leaving me alone. Amen.

I will ask the Father to send you the Holy Spirit who will help you and always be with you. The Spirit will show you what is true.

JOHN 14:16–17 CEV

Gentle Reminder

As a Christian, you have the most glorious privilege of being an example of Christ to everyone around you. You best do so by being humble, gentle, patient, and loving—just as God has been with you.

> **Be completely humble and gentle; be patient, bearing with one another in love.**
> EPHESIANS 4:2 NIV

Think of what that means for you today. You have the opportunity to remind others that there is a God who loves them dearly. And they will be attracted to him because of the qualities he shows through you.

Will you live as a worthy representative of God today—inviting him to be humble, patient, and loving through you—so that others can see God's true nature? Will you be his gentle reminder?

Dear God, I want to be a good and worthy example of your gentleness, humility, patience, and love. Work through me today. Amen.

Follow my example, as I follow the example of Christ.

1 CORINTHIANS 11:1 NIV

The One Who Defends You

Your defender is the gentle Lamb of God who takes away the sin of the world, but he is also the mighty warrior who defeats evil and administers justice. Though his powerful hand is worrisome for the enemy, he is always tender toward you.

Standing in the opened heaven, he surveys all that happens from an elevated perspective and takes in the complete picture of your life and struggles. A brilliant strategist and tactician, Jesus is devoted to you, his beloved, and honorably fulfills his promises.

> I saw heaven opened, and behold, a white horse, and He who sat on it is called Faithful and True.
>
> REVELATION 19:11
> NASB

Trust him—the one who defends you is faithful and true. He does everything in his power to help you—and it is *always* enough.

Dear God, you are faithful and true, my great defender. I praise you for your mighty and gentle hand that helps me today and every day. Amen.

Great and amazing are your deeds, O Lord God the Almighty! Just and true are your ways, O King of the nations! Who will not fear, O Lord, and glorify your name?

Revelation 15:3–4 ESV

Indelibly Engraved

It was a practice that was used by the Israelites during the time of Isaiah. In order to show their love or commitment to some important person or place, the people would permanently mark their hands.

> **I would not forget you! See, I have written your name on my hand.**
> ISAIAH 49:15–16 NLT

It is the sign God gives to you—engraving your name as a commitment to love and care for you. There is no way he could ever forget you.

In fact, God's thoughts are always turned toward you. So if you are feeling far from him this morning, remember his loving hands indelibly marked with your name. Then turn to him and allow him to engrave his name and comfort on your heart.

Dear God, thank you that my name is on your hand for all of eternity. You are most definitely written on my heart. Amen.

You will know
I am the Lord.
Anyone who
trusts in me
will not be
disappointed.
Isaiah 49:23 NCV

God Will Deliver You

Daniel was guilty of praying to God—in direct conflict with the Persian decree that people should pray to no one except the king. So Daniel was sentenced to the lions' den—certain death.

> **The king said to Daniel, May your God, Whom you are serving continually, deliver you!**
> DANIEL 6:16 AMP

Yet when morning came, Daniel had not been devoured. God had shut the mouths of the lions.

It seems an amazing story, but it is consistent with the character of God. When others punish you for being faithful to him, he does astounding things to help you—even saving you from the jaws of lions.

Serve him faithfully today, and do not fear what others will do. Your God will certainly deliver you in a marvelous way.

Dear God, you really do amaze me. Thank you that I can serve you faithfully with the assurance of your help and protection. Amen.

God rescues and saves people and does
mighty miracles in heaven and on
earth. He is the one who saved Daniel
from the power of the lions.

DANIEL 6:27 NCV

Without Fault

Spotless. Flawless. Holy. Without blemish. Beautiful. These are all words that describe you because of what Jesus has done.

It is often easier to believe the negative things people say than to keep a steady heart knowing that Christ has taken away your failings. Yet before you catalog your faults this morning, call this to mind—you are wonderfully created, beautifully forgiven, and absolutely flawless in God's sight.

> To him who is able to keep you from falling and to present you before his glorious presence without fault and with great joy.
>
> JUDE 1:24 NIV

Whatever others may say, whatever the world may prescribe, whatever you have been raised to believe, God looks at you with great joy. Praise him today for transforming you and bringing you into his presence without fault.

Dear God, thank you for accepting me completely without fault and with joy. To you be all the honor, glory, power, and praise. Amen.

He has reconciled you by His physical body through His death, to present you holy, faultless, and blameless before Him—if indeed you remain grounded and steadfast in the faith.

COLOSSIANS 1:22–23 HCSB

Endorsements

People respond to endorsements—they add credibility. So when Peter saw Jesus transfigured and conversing with Moses and Elijah, it was no wonder that he wanted others to see it too. Surely those two giants of the faith could convince others that Jesus was truly the Messiah.

> **This is My beloved Son, with whom I am well-pleased; listen to Him!**
> MATTHEW 17:5 NASB

Yet the only endorsement Jesus required was from God himself.

This is true for you as well. Though it is nice to have affirmation from others, you do not have to earn everyone's support. Especially when the only one you really need to please is God.

Today, seek to have God's approval. After all, his is the only endorsement that really counts.

Dear God, I want to be pleasing to you. Help me not to seek earthly endorsements but to live a life that gives you glory and joy. Amen.

Obviously, I'm not trying to be a people pleaser! No, I am trying to please God. If I were still trying to please people, I would not be Christ's servant.
GALATIANS 1:10 NLT

Expressing It to Him

Have you ever been so filled with wonder at the love and goodness of God that you burst out in praise to him? The Israelites did. They saw God take an impossible situation and turn it into a victory.

The powerful Egyptian army had pursued the Israelites and had trapped them at the Red Sea. The situation seemed hopeless. God not only provided a way out, but he also made sure that the Egyptians would never bother the Israelites again.

> **Bless the LORD, O my soul; and all that is within me, bless His holy name!**
>
> PSALM 103:1 NKJV

It is fitting to express gratefulness to God. Look for ways God is turning the impossible into a victory for you today, and thank him with all of your heart.

Dear God, thank you for working as powerfully today as you did for the Israelites. I praise you with thankfulness and joy. Amen.

The LORD is my strength and song,
and He has become my salvation; He
is my God, and I will praise Him; my
father's God, and I will exalt Him.

EXODUS 15:2 NKJV

Just As You Are

Have you ever been asked by a loved one to exaggerate your accomplishments or qualities in order to impress their colleagues or friends? It can be heartbreaking, because it can feel as if they do not accept you as you are.

However, you should never have to pretend in order to prove your love to another person. You do not have to act like someone different in order to be lovable. Real love always prefers the truth.

> **If you really love me . . .**
> GENESIS 20:13 CEV

God loves you and accepts you just as you are. This morning, rejoice that he brings out the best in you—who you were truly created to be—and that you never have to hide yourself from him.

Dear God, thank you that real love is about truth, and that you love me just as I am. Truly, you are good. Amen.

Your love is ever before me, and
I walk continually in your truth.
PSALM 26:3 NIV

Again I Say Rejoice!

Paul knew the amazing power of praise. He remembered being in the Philippian prison with Silas, his co-worker. Beaten and in chains, they sang hymns to God, knowing

> **Rejoice in the Lord always. Again I will say, rejoice!**
> PHILIPPIANS 4:4 NKJV

that their joy came from him and not from their circumstances. It was then that the doors of the prison flew open and they were freed.

That is why Paul knew that these words would be meaningful to the Philippians. They had seen it firsthand.

They are meaningful for you as well. Whatever your difficult situation, it does not control you. Your joy comes from God. So rejoice. Soon he will fling open the doors of your situation and set you free as well.

Dear God, I rejoice. My joy comes from you, and I praise you with gladness. Amen.

Let all who take refuge in you rejoice; let them ever sing for joy, and spread your protection over them, that those who love your name may exult in you.

PSALM 5:11 ESV

He Is Your Joy

God does not dwell on your mistakes. Rather, he faithfully turns away from anger in order to comfort and heal you. You are his joy.

He saves you from traps and schemes. Always trustworthy, he chases away all of your fears. He is your protector, defender, redeemer, savior, and friend. You are his joy.

> **Shout his praise with joy! For great is the Holy One of Israel who lives among you.**
> ISAIAH 12:6 NLT

He satisfies the deepest hungers of your soul. He teaches your heart with wisdom and nourishes your soul with his presence. You are his joy.

So praise God today for his goodness and might. Thank him that all your great blessings have come from his hand. Express your loving thoughts toward him—because he is *your* joy.

Dear God, you are my joy. I praise you for loving and protecting me. I glorify your name for your goodness to all your people. Amen.

Praise the LORD in song, for He has done
excellent things; let this be known
throughout the earth.

ISAIAH 12:5 NASB

Moments of Peace
for the Morning

Bless the LORD, O my soul; and all that
is within me, bless His holy name!

PSALM 103:1 NKJV

Streams of Tranquility

The soul often strives in vain after those things it cannot attain and which it cannot fulfill. Yet once your soul drinks of God, there is an endless supply of him to satisfy you. You never have to fear lack because God's Spirit is constantly ready to fill you with as much of God as you are able to receive.

> If anyone thirsts, let him come to Me and drink.
> JOHN 7:37 NKJV

Instead of the turmoil of running after fruitless earthly things, your soul finds rest and tranquility because it is filled to overflowing with the peace of God's Spirit. If you thirst today, drink deeply from the limitless stream of living water that will truly satisfy your soul.

Dear God, I am thirsty for you. Fill me to overflowing and give me peace today so that I may bring you glory. Amen.

Rivers of living water will brim and
spill out of the depths of anyone
who believes in me this way, just as
the Scripture says.

JOHN 7:38 MSG

Pray Believing

This morning, what is the main thing you pray for—the desire that you most hope to receive?

> **Whatever you ask for in prayer, believe (trust and be confident) that it is granted to you, and you will [get it].**
> MARK 11:24 AMP

It may seem far away and impossible. However, when you pray with faith, you acknowledge that God can solve any dilemma and that you fully trust him to help you.

As he answers, you follow his instructions with a humble spirit of hope. If your request is God's will, he will provide it. If it is not, he will change your desires to something better.

So pray expectantly, knowing that God loves to answer you. His response may not happen immediately, but be certain that he is moving mountains for you.

Dear God, I praise you for answering my prayers. I believe that you will either grant my request or provide something infinitely better. Amen.

If you have faith in God and don't doubt,
you can tell this mountain to get up and
jump into the sea, and it will.

MARK 11:23 CEV

A New Thing

Some days your heart will cry out for good news—some indication that you can be optimistic about the future. When God spoke the words to Isaiah, he was telling the prophet to look for the hope ahead. He says the same to you today.

> **I am doing a new thing; now it springs forth, do you not perceive it? I will make a way in the wilderness.**
> ISAIAH 43:19 ESV

The good news for you is that no matter what is going on in your life, God has the power, wisdom, and love to help you. He is doing something new today—whether you see it or not—providing new opportunities for you and endless possibilities. Giving you hope.

God is making a way in the wilderness for you. Look for it with a glad and hopeful heart.

Dear God, thank you for providing new opportunities and for giving me hope. I praise you for all the good things you are doing. Amen.

Praise God, the Father
of our Lord Jesus Christ.
God is so good, and by
raising Jesus from death,
he has given us new life
and a hope that lives on.

1 PETER 1:3 CEV

Mutual Encouragement

Paul was pleased that the Romans were growing in the faith—especially in a culture so opposed to Christianity. He had not met the people of the Roman church, but that did not take away from his concern for them. He knew they would benefit from his teaching and that he would gain by knowing them.

> **We may be mutually strengthened and encouraged and comforted by each other's faith.**
> ROMANS 1:12 AMP

This is the wonderful nature of the church. Its members exist for mutual encouragement. Believers can strengthen each other during difficult times with their various gifts.

You can be a blessing to other believers. Be willing to use your gifts so that others will be encouraged.

Dear God, thank you that believers can encourage each other. Please use my gifts today to strengthen, establish, and comfort others — and bring you glory. Amen.

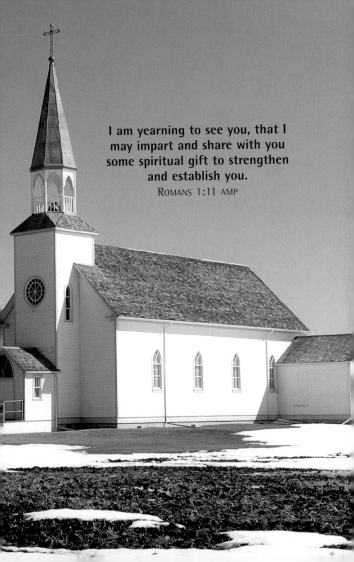

I am yearning to see you, that I may impart and share with you some spiritual gift to strengthen and establish you.

ROMANS 1:11 AMP

Even Under Siege

These are the difficult places—where the soul feels stifled and confined. You cannot find true safety there, but neither can you leave because to do so would expose you to more danger.

> **Blessed be the Lord! For He has shown me His marvelous loving favor when I was beset as in a besieged city.**
> PSALM 31:21 AMP

There is only one place to turn, and that is to your God. It is even in the times when you feel under siege that God's loving favor comforts you and makes you brave. That is when his voice is most powerful and encouraging, and his presence is most dear.

Are you besieged today? Then think of yourself closed in with God, and receive all the tender favor he desires to show you.

Dear God, you are powerful, kind, and good. Protect me on my way so that I might find my true safety and freedom in you. Amen.

Be of good courage, and He shall strengthen your heart, all you who hope in the LORD.

PSALM 31:24 NKJV

The Amazing Giver

How intimately he knows you—how amazing is his attention to every detail of your life. Your loving God knows the longings of your soul before you even ask.

Then why pray? you may wonder. Why persistently present your dearest requests before his throne?

> **Your Father knows what you need before you ask Him.**
> MATTHEW 6:8 NASB

Because it is in those times of prayer that *you* know *him*. He is not only hearing your request, but he is also inviting you to experience a close, profound relationship with him.

This morning as you pray, do not just go to God with an extensive list of requests. Go to him for his sake—the best gift of all. You will find how truly amazing he is.

Dear God, when I think of what my soul really longs for, it is you. Thank you for knowing my needs and for filling them so faithfully. Amen.

Praise be to God, who has not rejected my prayer or withheld his love from me!

PSALM 66:20 NIV

I Will See His Goodness

You can make it through today. Though your schedule may be full, though issues you face are difficult, and though you may not see the obstacles ahead, you can know for sure that you are going to be all right.

> **Yet I am confident that I will see the LORD's goodness while I am here in the land of the living.**
>
> PSALM 27:13 NLT

Why? Because God's goodness is with you, and he wants you to have joy. He will comfort you during the difficult moments, and he will strengthen you for whatever challenges come your way.

No matter what today holds, God is with you—to love you and help you through it. Put your confidence in him and take notice of all the ways he shows you his goodness.

Dear God, I am confident that I will see your goodness today. Thank you for showing me your goodness in every situation. Amen.

Surely your goodness and love
will be with me all my life.

PSALM 23:6 NCV

His Good Name

God instructed Moses to teach the Israelites his name—*I Am Who I Am*.

However, the Hebrew language is different from modern languages because it does not indicate a sense of time. His name could just as easily be translated *I Am Who I Have Been* or *I Will Forever Be Who I Am Now*.

> You, O GOD my Lord, deal on my behalf for your name's sake; because your steadfast love is good, deliver me!
>
> PSALM 109:21 ESV

God is consistent and holy. Because his name indicates his character, you can trust him to help you as he has always helped those who love him.

Therefore, take heart today with the assurance that the God who so faithfully provided for Moses will provide for you today.

Dear God, I take comfort that your name indicates a consistent, faithful character. I know that those who have trusted in you have never been disappointed. Amen.

I will praise you forever for what you have done; in your name I will hope, for your name is good. I will praise you in the presence of your saints.

PSALM 52:9 NIV

The Gentle Shepherd

God is the kind of good and gentle shepherd with which a flock will undoubtedly thrive. He knows his sheep—he provides for and nurtures them with knowledge and understanding. He guides them past any dangers to places of rest.

He defends them with his skill and robust strength—gladly giving his life rather than seeing one fall to a foe. Gently and mercifully he attends to each one from birth to death—assuring that each one has a good life and receives joyful rewards.

> **The LORD is my shepherd.**
> PSALM 23:1 NKJV

Truly, this gentle shepherd is good. He is *your* shepherd, your God. Claim him as your own, for surely, with him, you shall never want.

Dear God, you are my gentle shepherd. Today, I thank you that your goodness and mercy are with me all the days of my life. Amen.

They will lie down in pleasant places and feed in lush mountain pastures. I myself will tend my sheep and cause them to lie down in peace, says the Sovereign LORD.

Ezekiel 34:14–15 NLT

His Will Be Done

It is a simple refrain as you begin your day—*Lord, your will be done*. It was the humble attitude of heart and willingness to obey that Jesus exhibited as he opened the way to God for every person.

> **Father, if You are willing, remove this cup from Me; yet not My will, but [always] Yours be done.**
> LUKE 22:42 AMP

You are called to the same—agreeing with God in good times and bad because only he can make you truly happy. You count his plans more wonderful, more profoundly satisfying, and infinitely wiser than your own.

Make this your song today—*Lord, your will be done*. It will fill your life with such a beautiful melody of gentleness and grace that both you and those around you will be eternally changed.

Dear God, whether it is difficult or easy, I want to do as you ask. I know that above all, your plans are best. Amen.

The world and everything in it that people
desire is passing away; but those who
do the will of God live forever.

1 John 2:17 GNT

Purely the Truth

You can only put your trust in something that is completely true—and the Bible has proven absolutely faithful throughout history. Certainly, there are things that have yet to be seen—such as the second coming of Christ and what life will be like in heaven. Nevertheless, you can know that everything you see is evidence for all you have not yet seen.

> **God never tells a lie! So, at the proper time, God our Savior gave this message and told me to announce what he had said.**
> TITUS 1:2–3 CEV

God does not lie. He cannot mislead you. His holiness absolutely prevents it. What he communicates to you about your life, the world, and eternity is unquestionably true.

You can count on God to be honest, so trust him today with whatever comes.

Dear God, I praise you for telling the truth—and being the truth. I trust you to lead me because you are absolutely honest and faithful. Amen.

God is not like people, who lie; He is
not a human who changes his mind.
Whatever he promises, he does; He
speaks, and it is done.

NUMBERS 23:19 GNT

A Secure Hold

An anchor holds a ship in place even when waves, winds, and currents try to move it. In the same way, Jesus holds you securely to the Father though life, trials, and cultural tides may buffet you.

> **This hope we have as an anchor of the soul, both sure and steadfast.**
> HEBREWS 6:19 NKJV

Jesus is the constant connection between you and the Father—always representing you to him, and helping you to understand what he is doing. He is the perfect minister to your soul because he provides unbroken communication between you and your Creator.

Jesus never waivers—even when everything around you is sinking. Therefore, take this hope as an anchor for your soul today—Jesus has a secure hold on you. And because of him, you have smooth sailing with God.

Dear God, thank you that I don't have to drown in my circumstances, because you are my sure anchor. I praise you. Amen.

Christ has entered, not into holy places made with hands, which are copies of the true things, but into heaven itself, now to appear in the presence of God on our behalf.

HEBREWS 9:24 ESV

So That It Go Well

The purpose of obedience is twofold. Though you never have to obey God to earn his love—that is always given freely—you obey him because he is, in fact, God. He is your Lord, and it is good to express your thanks to him by doing as he says.

> **Do what is right and good in the sight of the LORD, that it may be well with you.**
>
> DEUTERONOMY 6:18
> NKJV

There is a second purpose for obedience. As you follow God, he positions you perfectly to receive the deepest desires of your heart. He blesses you—and no one knows how to give you joy like God does.

Obedience is not only about thankfulness but also about doing what is best for your life. Therefore, today, obey him gladly, and everything will go well for you.

Dear God, obedience is difficult at times. Please help me to obey so that I may show my thankfulness and fully receive your great blessings. Amen.

The LORD our God commanded us to obey all these laws and to fear him for our own prosperity and well-being, as is now the case.

DEUTERONOMY 6:24 NLT

Remember the Dry Ground

God commanded the priests to carry the ark into the Jordan's rushing floodwaters. As their feet touched the river's edge, the waters piled up.

To Joshua and Caleb—who had been present forty years earlier—this was remarkably similar to when God parted the Red Sea and helped them escape from Egypt. The memory of that dry ground between the waters gave them courage to go forward.

> **As soon as the feet of the priests who were carrying the Ark touched the water at the river's edge, the water began piling up.**
>
> JOSHUA 3:15–16 NLT

When God asks you to step out in faith, he often brings some memory of past faithfulness to help you. As you face challenges today, remember how God has parted the waters for you—and trust him to lead safely.

Dear God, you have always helped me. Help me to step out in faith by reminding me of how trustworthy you have been in the past. Amen.

The LORD your God caused the water to stop flowing until you finished crossing it, just as the LORD did to the Red Sea. . . . The LORD did this so all people would know he has great power.

JOSHUA 4:23–24 NCV

Moments of Peace
for the Morning

Yet I am confident that I will see the LORD's goodness while I am here in the land of the living.

PSALM 27:13 NLT

Such Love

From birth, Nicodemus was raised as a Pharisee—living in obedience to the law. Every day he said the prayers and performed the rituals that would keep him right before God. It was a tedious life.

Nicodemus learned that God wanted more than just obedience to laws and regulations—God wanted a genuine relationship based on love.

> God so greatly loved and dearly prized the world that He [even] gave up His only begotten (unique) Son.
> JOHN 3:16 AMP

You may think that in order to know God, you have to do certain things. Yet Jesus has already done everything necessary for you to be close to God. His love never binds you unmercifully to regulations or rituals. His love sets you free so you can love him in return.

Dear God, I love you. Thank you for doing so much to have a genuine love relationship with me. You are truly wonderful. Amen.

He had always loved those in the
world who were his own, and he
loved them to the very end.

JOHN 13:1 GNT

No Fear in Love

The apostle John knew the security of Jesus' love firsthand. He had seen his worst fears confirmed at the crucifixion but utterly defeated at the resurrection.

Years later, John daily experienced persecution. Yet he affirmed that as long as he had Jesus' love, there was no reason to be afraid. Fear, after all, is based in punishment. And how could anyone truly hurt him as long as the resurrected Jesus protected him? Who could possibly stand against the God who had overcome death?

> There is no fear in love; instead, perfect love drives out fear.
> 1 JOHN 4:18 HCSB

When you belong to God, you never have to fear. He is stronger than any foe you could face, and his perfect love will always protect you.

Dear God, thank you for protecting me with your wonderful love and your mighty power. Truly, I have no reason to fear. Amen.

We can confidently say, "The Lord is my helper; I will not fear; what can man do to me?"

HEBREWS 13:6 ESV

A Spring of Strength

Ezra read from the Book of the Law—the record of God's past faithfulness. Though the people were humbled by the stories, they were inspired to celebrate the wonderful God they served.

God's joy is in his interaction with you and all those who have loved him throughout history. Scripture tells of his faithfulness and forgiveness—how he gladly provided for his people and delighted in helping them.

> **The joy of the LORD is your strength.**
> NEHEMIAH 8:10 NASB

Studying the Bible and discovering how he has acted in others' lives will be a spring of encouragement and gladness for you. This morning, celebrate the great gift you have been given in the Bible, and take strength from reading about his joy.

Dear God, I praise you for your wonderful interaction with people recorded in Scripture. It gives me great strength knowing that I am your joy. Amen.

All the people went away to eat, to drink, to send portions and to celebrate a great festival, because they understood the words which had been made known to them.

NEHEMIAH 8:12 NASB

Discouraged?

Every morning, you have an option. You can either choose to be discouraged or choose to hope. This is an especially difficult choice if you have not slept well, are sick, or face a busy day full of challenges. It is a decision that remains in your power.

> **Why are you cast down, O my soul, and why are you in turmoil within me? Hope in God.**
> Psalm 42:11 esv

You can govern your attitude—especially when meditating on the God who can turn everything around for you. Your circumstances need not dictate your mood.

You will find that when you choose your attitude, you will be better able to affect how your day turns out.

Are you discouraged this morning? Put your hope in God. He will certainly bless your soul.

Dear God, with you the choice is easy. Help me to center my hope on you so that I will have a good attitude today. Amen.

Why must I go about mourning . . . ? Send forth your light and your truth, let them guide me; let them bring me to your holy mountain, to the place where you dwell.

PSALM 43:2-3 NIV

Peace Through Faith

She had tried everything, but nothing could rid her of the infirmity she had endured for over a decade. When she heard that Jesus was close by, she went to see him. She knew that if she could just touch the remarkable man of God, she would be healed.

> **Your faith has made you well; go in peace.**
> LUKE 8:48 NASB

Many people crowded in on Jesus that day, but only that woman touched him with her faith. And because of it Jesus' power was released, and the woman received peace from her illness.

Believing is the key to peace. Today, reach out to God in faith and hold on to him. He will give you rest from whatever troubles your soul.

Dear God, you know what hurts my heart. I truly believe that you can help me. Thank you for your lovely peace. Amen.

Only God gives inward peace,
and I depend on him.
PSALM 62:5 CEV

Blessed Is the Believer

There is so much peace in simply believing, and just knowing that God will do as he said.

Even at her young age, Mary understood that. Perhaps that is the reason God chose to bless her with being the mother of the Messiah—because her faith was so strong.

> You are blessed, because you believed that the Lord would do what he said.
> LUKE 1:45 NLT

Certainly, it is not always easy to simply rest in God's promises. Your mind will strive to think of every obstacle that could impede you.

When you believe—really fully trust—that God will do as he says, you will experience a deep, abiding peace that will truly bless you. You will know his presence and power in a way that will amaze everyone.

Dear God, I want to have Mary's faith, the kind that believes the impossible. Thank you for blessing and strengthening my faith. Amen.

My soul magnifies the Lord, and my spirit has rejoiced in God my Savior. For He has regarded the lowly state of His maidservant; for behold, henceforth all generations will call me blessed.

LUKE 1:46–48 NKJV

In the Stillness

The hurly-burly pace of your life can leave you tired and discouraged if you have no oasis of rest. That is why a relationship with God is so poignant.

He is the great well of peace and strength from which you can always draw. You must drop your concerns at his feet and abandon your right to worry about them.

> **Be still, and know that I am God.**
> Psalm 46:10 NKJV

Be still before him and relax. He can handle all of it.

It is in the stillness of your heart that God's power protects you in times of turmoil. And it is in that quietness that you will have the patience and endurance for everything that comes your way today.

Dear God, before the day gets going, help me to be still before you. Fill me with your peace and strength and I will praise your name. Amen.

God is our shelter and strength, always ready to help in times of trouble. So we will not be afraid, even if the earth is shaken and mountains fall into the ocean depths.

PSALM 46:1–2 GNT

A Good Crop

There was a farmer who went out to plant seed. However, birds and wind took some seed away; and thorns and stones choked even more seed. Yet there was also good seed that properly took root and grew.

Jesus explained that the seed is the word of God—and if it finds a fertile place in your heart, it produces a wonderful result.

> These are the ones who, having heard the word with an honest and good heart, hold on to it and by enduring, bear fruit.
> LUKE 8:15 HCSB

No harvest grows up overnight—every good fruit has its time. This is why it is important for you to be patient with the effect the Bible has on your life. You may not be able to see it grow, but it is certainly producing a good crop in you.

Dear God, thank you that if I remain consistent with studying the Bible, you will produce wonderful things in me. Please help me to be patient. Amen.

The rest of the seeds fell on good ground where they grew and produced a hundred times as many seeds.

LUKE 8:8 CEV

Impacting the World

Sometimes it may seem as if you are not making a meaningful impact. Your daily routine feels unimportant—especially with everything happening in the world. You wonder if you could do more with the life God has given you.

> **You obey the law of Christ when you offer each other a helping hand.**
> GALATIANS 6:2 CEV

D. L. Moody wrote, "He does the most for God's great world who does the best in his own little world."

All around you are people who could be wonderfully affected by your help and kindness. God asks you to have an impact on the world by loving them as he loves them.

The most meaningful work you can do is to care for the people around you. Will you do it?

Dear God, show me someone to help today. Thank you that I can truly impact the world by loving people the way you love them. Amen.

Through love you should serve one another.
GALATIANS 5:13 AMP

The Face of Forgiveness

Jacob had feared this meeting for years. He knew he had treated his brother Esau badly—stealing his blessing and tricking him into forfeiting his birthright. Esau had every right to detest him.

> **If now I have found favor in your sight, then take my present from my hand, for I see your face as one sees the face of God.**
> GENESIS 33:10 NASB

Yet when Esau saw Jacob, he ran to him—hugged and kissed him. To Jacob, knowing that Esau forgave him was like seeing the face of God.

Is there someone in your life whom you need to forgive? No doubt, it is difficult to do. God can give you the grace to embrace and pardon that person. In doing so, you set both of you free from the past. Undoubtedly, God will shine through your forgiving face.

Dear God, this is tough, but I know that I will feel better after I forgive. May this person see your face shining through me. Amen.

When people sin, you should forgive
and comfort them, so they won't give
up in despair. You should make them
sure of your love for them.

2 CORINTHIANS 2:7–8 CEV

The Sacred and the Sifting

Sifting—the shaking of wheat until it separates. You know what it is like—to be strained to the point that everything falls apart.

> Satan has asked for you, that he may sift you as wheat. But I have prayed for you, that your faith should not fail.
>
> LUKE 22:31–32 NKJV

Though it is not strange that you are sifted, it is amazing who is praying for you. Your intercessor is Jesus—who defends you and walks with you daily. Can you imagine the power and insightfulness of Jesus' prayers?

It is in the sifting that you experience the sacred because you receive Jesus' very thoughts concerning you. And so, instead of shaking apart, you become one with him.

Today, remember that God the Son is praying for you. Then your faith will not fail, but will remain strong and hopeful in him.

Dear God, thank you for praying for me. I know I can make it through anything with you as my defender and constant friend. Amen.

Holy Father, keep them safe by the power of
your name, the name you gave me, so that
they will be one, just as you and I are one.

JOHN 17:11 NCV

Of Silver and Gold

To make gold and silver fit for use, they must be put to the fire. This process serves to both remove their impurities and make the precious metals malleable.

God prepares you and makes you ready for service in much the same way. In the heat and pressure of everyday life, God burns away all the things that hinder you from serving him, and he molds you into someone who truly shines with his love.

I will bring the third part through the fire, and will refine them as silver is refined and will test them as gold is tested.

ZECHARIAH 13:9 AMP

Has God turned up the heat in your life today? Take heart—he sees something truly valuable and beautiful in you, and he has allowed the fire for the refining of your soul.

Dear God, thank you for valuing me so greatly. Please help me to endure the heat in my life so I can truly shine for you. Amen.

The LORD their God will
save them on that day as
the flock of His people;
for they are like jewels in
a crown, sparkling
over His land.

ZECHARIAH 9:16 HCSB

So Real to Me

The book of Job is full of theories and theologies. The questions abound. Why do good people suffer? Is God punishing Job for some wrong action? Shouldn't people who trust in God prosper?

> **I admit I once lived by rumors of you; now I have it all firsthand—from my own eyes and ears!**
> JOB 42:5 MSG

God's desire is not for you to form hypotheses about him. Rather, God wants you to really trust him—and it is only when you allow yourself to be vulnerable that you can experience him fully.

After all of his suffering, Job was able to say that God was real to him, more personal than he could have imagined. And it filled him with joy.

Today, set your heart on really knowing God instead of just knowing *about* him.

Dear God, I want to really know you. Help me to be vulnerable with you so that I can experience you fully in every situation. Amen.

I will see him for myself, and
I long for that moment.
JOB 19:27 CEV

An Excellent Guide

If you desire to be taught this morning—you are willing to accept God's counsel and acknowledge it as superior to your own—then you fulfill the requirements for him to lead you.

As chaplain Thomas Goodwin wrote, "The Lord will teach the humble his secrets, he will not teach proud scholars."

> **He leads the humble in what is right, and the humble He teaches His way.**
> PSALM 25:9 AMP

God speaks to your listening soul, showing you his ways step by step. He leads you in an adventure of discovery and understanding, and he sets a purposeful course that brings him glory and you satisfaction.

It is good that you have humbled yourself to God this morning. Listen to him, and he will share his most excellent secrets with you.

Dear God, I want your counsel and acknowledge that your wisdom is far greater than my own. Teach me your magnificent ways. Amen.

Lead me by your truth and teach me,
for you are the God who saves me.
All day long I put my hope in you.

PSALM 25:5 NLT

Moments of Peace for the Morning

You are blessed, because you
believed that the Lord would
do what he said.

LUKE 1:45 NLT

A Flawless Record

God promised childless centenarian Abraham that his offspring would be as numerous as the stars. He guaranteed that they would have a land of their own—but only after a four-hundred-year captivity in Egypt. And he assured Moses that he would lead those two million-plus descendants of Abraham out of Egypt, and back to the land they were pledged.

> Not a word failed of any good thing which the LORD had spoken to the house of Israel. All came to pass.
>
> JOSHUA 21:45 NKJV

Standing in that Promised Land, Abraham's descendants knew that God had faithfully kept *all* those vows and more.

Throughout Israel's history, God pledged some really amazing things—and he delivered *every one*. His record on promise keeping is flawless. Therefore, whatever he has assured you of is no problem whatsoever. Trust him.

Dear God, I praise you that not one word of your promises has ever failed. Amen.

It is the LORD your God who fights for you, just as he promised you. Be very careful, therefore, to love the LORD your God.

JOSHUA 23:10–11 ESV

A Faithful Bridge Builder

How can a God who is limitless in power, wisdom, and love understand what it is like to live in your world? Though he created it, does he know how frustrating and frightening it can be? Though he knows the thoughts and heart of every person, can he understand how raw emotions feel? Can he know human pain or the fear of facing death?

> **It was necessary for Jesus to be in every respect like us . . . so that he could be our merciful and faithful High Priest before God.**
>
> HEBREWS 2:17 NLT

The answer is *yes*, because Jesus came to connect the expanse between you and God. The bridge he builds between God and your humanity is also the path for you to know God. Jesus completely understands both, and he serves as the perfect mediator. He is wonderful, isn't he?

Dear God, it is hard to understand all you have done for me, but I am so thankful that you understand me perfectly. Amen.

In bringing many sons to glory, it was fitting that God, for whom and through whom everything exists, should make the author of their salvation perfect through suffering.

HEBREWS 2:10 NIV

An Inner Preparation

It is difficult to be disciplined when there is no goal ahead. Yet you have a wonderful goal—a great and high calling.

> **Get your minds ready for action, being self-disciplined, and set your hope completely on the grace to be brought to you at the revelation of Jesus Christ**
> 1 PETER 1:13 HCSB

Peter taught that before his time, the prophets looked forward to Messiah's coming. They searched out all of the details regarding the Messiah so that they would be ready for him.

Now that Jesus has come and has provided salvation, you also are to study his life and allow God's Spirit to prepare you to see him.

Whether it is in heaven or by his second coming here on earth, get yourself ready to greet God today by being disciplined in learning about him.

Dear God, how wonderful that I get to see you. Help me to be disciplined so that I'll be prepared when I meet you face-to-face. Amen.

You are receiving the goal of your
faith, the salvation of your souls.

1 PETER 1:9 HCSB

With Your Head Held High

This morning, you have been set free. You are no longer a captive. You have been released from wrongdoing, fear, and guilt.

Is that how you are living?

God has freed you in order to inspire the highest within you. Certainly, there are guidelines in that—but they do not oppress or hurt your spirit. Rather, they are the kind of disciplines that Olympic hopefuls have—those that stretch you to be your very best and help you reach your greatest aspirations.

> I have set you free; now walk with your heads held high.
> LEVITICUS 26:13 CEV

You have been released to be the finest you possible. Therefore, go with your head held high, knowing that God is with you and he has set you free.

Dear God, thank you for setting me free. I will live with my head held high—being the best me I can be for your glory. Amen.

I will look on you with favor
and make you fruitful.
LEVITICUS 26:9 NIV

A Good Future

It wasn't in the midst of a peaceful time that God spoke these words to Jeremiah—it was as the nation of Judah faced a seventy-year captivity in Babylon. Yet God faithfully fulfilled his promise to bring them back to their homeland and to give them a good future.

> **"I know the plans I have for you,"** declares the LORD . . . **"plans to give you hope and a future."**
> JEREMIAH 29:11 NIV

Though unfortunate things will happen in your life, God is with you, and his plans for you are filled with hope. You don't have to fear the future or worry that you'll be stuck in your situation forever.

God used those years to teach Judah to trust him. He is teaching you, too. Believe him. He is faithful to help you with whatever happens today.

Thank you, God, for giving me a wonderful future and for teaching me to trust you more. I look forward to your excellent plans. Amen.

"Don't let your eyes fill with tears.
You will be rewarded for your
work!" says the LORD . . . "There is
hope for you in the future."

JEREMIAH 31:16–17 NCV

Like the Eagle

It has been observed that an eagle will slowly hold back from feeding its chicks in order to get them to fly. The adult will appeal to its hungry children with tasty morsels so that—as the parent swoops up into the sky—the eaglets will catch the updraft and take flight.

> **He was like an eagle hovering over its nest, overshadowing its young, then spreading its wings, lifting them into the air, teaching them to fly.**
>
> DEUTERONOMY 32:11
> MSG

God works in much the same way. He allows there to be some hunger in your life so that you will step out and seek him. As you step out in faith to follow him, he bears you up on his wings of faithfulness and love, and teaches you to soar.

Mighty God, thank you for teaching me to fly. Thank you that even the needs in my life are your wonderful way of instructing me. Amen.

He will cover you with His pinions, and under His wings shall you trust and find refuge; His truth and His faithfulness are a shield and a buckler.

PSALM 91:4 AMP

No Eye Has Seen

Your imagination is capable of great things—yet it is no match for God's. Your thoughts may reach high, but God's good plans for you are infinitely higher.

> **No eye has seen, no ear has heard, no mind has conceived what God has prepared for those who love him.**
>
> 1 CORINTHIANS 2:9 NIV

Whatever it is you dream about, it may seem marvelous—quite certain to make you happy. Yet God wants to increase your wonder and joy by creating something extraordinary.

God wants you to be so amazed at what he does that any memory of hardship fades away and you spontaneously praise him.

Today, therefore, do not fret about what your eyes haven't seen. Rather, thank him for it—knowing that what is ahead is sure to be out of this world.

Dear God, what amazing things have you prepared for me? I will praise you today knowing that it is better than anything I could possibly imagine. Amen.

You did awesome things beyond our highest expectations. And oh, how the mountains quaked!

ISAIAH 64:3 NLT

Then I Am Strong

You know your weaknesses—and perhaps you regret them. However, they are the very areas through which God can perform miraculously.

Conversely, when you have exceptional talents and assets, you can fall into the trap of thinking you do not need God.

> **For Christ's sake, I delight in weaknesses, in insults, in hardships, in persecutions, in difficulties. For when I am weak, then I am strong.**
> 2 CORINTHIANS 12:10 NIV

Though he can work through you when you acknowledge you need him, it is a different story when you believe you can accomplish everything by yourself. Then he must teach you that his good plans are achieved only through his power.

So don't worry about your weaknesses today. They are wonderful opportunities for God to show you his glory.

Dear God, I praise you for my weaknesses. Thank you for achieving your great plans and showing me your glory through them. Amen.

If I must boast, I
would rather boast
about the things
that show how
weak I am. God, the
Father of our Lord
Jesus, who is to be
praised forever,
knows I tell
the truth.

2 CORINTHIANS 11:30–31
NLT

Write It Down

Journaling is a wonderfully encouraging activity. As you pray and read the Bible, you record your concerns, what you learn, and how God answers you. It becomes a record of your communication with him.

> Then the LORD replied: "Write down the revelation and make it plain on tablets."
>
> HABAKKUK 2:2 NIV

There is something about seeing his words to you formed on paper that somehow makes them more real—more possible. You document God's personal promises to you, and the certainty of them gives you peace. And if you ever begin to doubt, you can always go back and read them again.

This morning, write down what you learn during your time alone with God. He will certainly bless you through it.

Dear God, help me to write down what you want for me to remember. Thank you for making your promises real to me through the written word. Amen.

Write the things which you have seen, and the things which are, and the things which will take place after these things.

REVELATION 1:19 NASB

Not Because of Your Merit

God was forthright with the people of Israel. He did not choose them because of any merit of their own. He chose them because he loved them and had made a covenant with their ancestors.

> **He did it out of sheer love, keeping the promise he made to your ancestors.**
>
> DEUTERONOMY 7:8
> MSG

It is a humbling thing to be accepted by God because of his great love for you. Yet it should also give you peace. Because you did not earn it, you cannot lose it. Because his love is unconditional, there is nothing you can do to mess it up.

It is not by your strength, beauty, brilliance, or talent that you gain God's acceptance. He just loves you for who you are. Today, love him back.

Dear God, I do love you back. Thank you for the peace and joy that come from your marvelous, unconditional love. Amen.

GOD, your God, chose you out of all the
people on Earth for himself as a cherished,
personal treasure. GOD wasn't attracted to
you and didn't choose you because you
were big and important.

DEUTERONOMY 7:6–7 MSG

A Promise Proven True

Everyone wanted to see the great deliverer that God had promised to send. Yet Simeon had God's special assurance that he would meet him.

As time went by, perhaps Simeon wondered if he had heard God correctly—would he live long enough to meet the deliverer? However, he obediently went to the temple whenever God moved him. And on one very special day, the promise was proven true—Simeon met Jesus.

> **The Holy Spirit had shown him that he would see the Messiah of God before he died.**
> LUKE 2:26 MSG

You may have a promise that has been long in coming. You wonder whether you heard God—or just the loud longings of your heart.

Today, be obedient to God, and you likewise will see his promises to you proven true.

Dear God, thank you that all your promises to me are true. Help me to be patient until you faithfully fulfill them. Amen.

Simeon . . . took the child in his arms and praised God, saying, "Lord, now I can die in peace! As you promised me, I have seen the Savior."

LUKE 2:28–30 NLT

Fully Assured

Here is the definition of faith for you to live by today—being completely assured of what you hope for and absolutely certain of what you do not see. Though everything around you goes against that hope, you have complete confidence in God.

> **Faith is the assurance of things hoped for, the conviction of things not seen.**
> HEBREWS 11:1 NASB

You believe in God and that he can do the impossible. Perhaps the lingering question is, will he? Does God love you enough to help you?

The answer is absolutely *yes*. Even though God has shown his love for you in Christ, you still must accept his love by faith, fully assured that he will not fail you.

Therefore, have strong faith today in the wonderful God who loves you.

Dear God, not only do I believe you exist and can do anything, but also I completely trust that you love me enough to help me. Amen.

May the Lord direct your hearts into [realizing and showing] the love of God and into the steadfastness and patience of Christ.

2 THESSALONIANS 3:5 AMP

The Least and Him

It is extraordinary to realize how closely Jesus relates to the neediest people. His association is so intimate and sincere that you are promised that whatever good you do for them, you do for him.

This is because Jesus could look into people's lives and thoroughly know their deepest needs—whether for food and shelter or for healing and forgiveness. Perhaps it is because his empathy is so profound that he so greatly appreciates your service on their behalf.

> **Whatever you did for one of the least of these brothers of Mine, you did for Me.**
> MATTHEW 25:40 HCSB

When you compassionately see a person's need, you are not only acting *for* Jesus, but you are also acting *like* Jesus. You relate out of mercy and react just as he would.

Dear God, thank you for your mercy to me. Help me to meet others' needs with your sincere compassion and profound sympathy. Amen.

I was naked and you clothed me, I was sick and you visited me, I was in prison and you came to me.

MATTHEW 25:36 ESV

A Beautiful Message

People need hope. They try to find it in many things, but the only real and lasting hope is in God. That is why it is wonderful to be his representative.

Most people have a distorted perception of God—either as a controlling taskmaster or an impersonal being that does not bother to intervene. Yet you know who he really is—the God who gives joy and eternal life.

> **How beautiful on the mountains are the feet of those who bring good news of peace and salvation.**
>
> ISAIAH 52:7 NLT

Today, tell others the beautiful message of the God of hope so that they can experience his peace and salvation as well. You will find their gratitude is utterly overwhelming when they finally meet and embrace the God they've longed to know.

Dear God, I praise you for your beautiful message. Help me to repeat it to those who need hope so they may know you as well. Amen.

Your watchmen lift up their voices; together they sing for joy; for they shall see eye to eye the return of the Lord to Zion.

ISAIAH 52:8 AMP

Moments of Peace
for the Morning

Be still, and know that I am God.

Psalm 46:10 NKJV

Setting the Standard

The churches on the island of Crete badly needed leaders. Interestingly, when the apostle Paul wrote to help them, he did not require that potential teachers have an impressive scope of knowledge. Rather, he advised that what was truly essential was that they be people of good character.

> **In everything set them an example by doing what is good.**
> TITUS 2:7 NIV

Though knowledge is important, you teach others most by your example. It is crucial that others observe how the godly life is lived out rather than just to talk about it.

Today, teach those around you by being self-controlled, having integrity, and being eager to do good. People will see the standard you set and will be attracted to the God you serve.

Dear God, help me to do good and to have good character, self-control, and integrity and so that others will be drawn to you. Amen.

Give special emphasis to these matters, so that those who believe in God may be concerned with giving their time to doing good deeds, which are good and useful for everyone.

TITUS 3:8 GNT

Bringing Out the Best

A knife is sharpened by whetting it with another piece of iron—generally with a parallel movement. However, if you set the knife contrary to the other metal—striking edge to edge, you will dull, damage, or even break the blade.

> **Iron sharpens iron, and one man sharpens another.**
> PROVERBS 27:17 HCSB

The principle is the same for your relationships. If your companions are living contrary to God, they can hurt your relationship with him. However, if your closest friends are on a parallel course in knowing God, you will sharpen and bring out the best in each other.

Do your dearest friends hone your relationship with God—or turn you away from him? Today, seek buddies who will encourage you to be your best for God.

Dear God, help me to find friends who will help me grow in you—and to be a friend to those who need you. Amen.

I am a friend to all who fear You, to those who keep Your precepts.

PSALM 119:63 HCSB

Keep Watch With Me

Jesus experienced agonizing sorrow in the Garden of Gethsemane. His disciples could neither understand nor share it with him. Jesus asked them to stay nearby because their presence and prayers comforted to him.

> **My soul is exceedingly sorrowful, even to death. Stay here and watch with Me.**
>
> MATTHEW 26:38 NKJV

It is hard to know what to say to a loved one who is suffering. You know their heart is breaking, and you want to help. Yet what can you do?

You can express your love for them by just being near. Your presence comforts them and shows them they are not alone—even if you cannot share their burden.

Today, don't fall asleep on your loved ones. Keep watch with them during their time of need.

Dear God, you know exactly what my loved ones need. I will sit with them and pray—please make me a comfort to them. Amen.

They came to a place named Gethsemane; and [Jesus] said to His disciples, "Sit here until I have prayed."

MARK 14:32 NASB

Seasoned With Grace

Salt is useful for many reasons. Not only does it make food tasty—it also acts as a preservative and purifier. The same is true when grace is applied to your speech.

God does amazing things to your words. He prepares them to be appetizing to the person listening. He makes them preservative—giving them lasting beneficial value. And he purifies them—assuring that they will be safely received.

> Let your speech always be gracious, seasoned with salt, so that you may know how you ought to answer each person.
>
> COLOSSIANS 4:6 ESV

You never know when something you say will touch a person's heart. However, when your speech has been seasoned with God's grace, you know that your words will be a feast for the hearer.

Dear God, thank you for making my words appetizing, preservative, and pure by your grace. I pray that they will bring you glory. Amen.

The right words will be there. The Holy Spirit will give you the right words when the time comes.

LUKE 12:12 MSG

Bound by Love and Faithfulness

Two things are given for you to write upon your heart this morning—*love* and *faithfulness*. If you embrace them with your whole being, they will define your character and course.

> **Let love and faithfulness never leave you. . . . Then you will win favor and a good name in the sight of God and man.**
> PROVERBS 3:3–4 NIV

Show your love by being kind and compassionate to others, and by trusting and worshiping your God. Prove your faithfulness by exercising integrity and being honest in all of your dealings, fully obedient and loyal to God's word.

You have been promised that if you are bound by love and faithfulness you will be respected by others and blessed by God. Truly a wonderful way to spend your day, indeed.

Dear God, bind love and faithfulness to me. Make them permeate my character and future so that I will, indeed, win favor with you and others. Amen.

Loving-kindness and mercy, loyalty
and faithfulness, shall be to those
who devise good.

PROVERBS 14:22 AMP

His Steadfast Love

Because of the Lord's unwavering love for you, this morning brings a brand-new sunrise—unlike any that has ever been before. It lights a world brimming with creative ways in which God shows himself to you.

From the early hues of the sky to the birds that fly in it, he has painted them for you. From the bounty of the ocean to the harvest of the field, he tirelessly brings

> **The earth is full of the steadfast love of the LORD.**
> PSALM 33:5 ESV

them forth to show you his unfailing provision.

He does not grow fatigued of watching over and protecting you. He never grows weary of your prayers. Rather, his enduring joy is showing you his steadfast love through all the wonders of creation.

Dear God, of all the wonders of this world, you are more wonderful than them all. Thank you for your unwavering love. Amen.

The LORD watches over those who obey him, those who trust in his constant love . . . We put our hope in the LORD; he is our protector and our help.

PSALM 33:18, 20 GNT

Mandatory Barriers

Can you imagine if there were no shorelines to contain the oceans or rivers? If you have ever experienced a flood, you know the devastation that rushing waters can cause. Can you imagine how difficult life would be if the tides were not at least somewhat predictable?

> **Why aren't you in awe before me? Yes, me, who made the shorelines to contain the ocean waters.**
> JEREMIAH 5:22 MSG

Throughout the natural world there are barriers that separate land, sea, sky, and space, barriers that keep the world working and in order. God provides you with boundaries as well, principles that help you remain safe, happy, and free from disaster.

God gives you his decrees to protect you. Approach him in awe today, and thank him for keeping your world in working order.

Dear God, you truly amaze me. Even if I don't understand your principles, I know you work through them to protect me from danger. Amen.

The boundary lines have fallen for
me in pleasant places; indeed,
I have a beautiful inheritance.

PSALM 16:6 HCSB

Seeing the Power of God

Had he been an ordinary man, his lifeless, bleeding body on the cross may have inspired grief and perhaps disgust—but certainly not awe. Yet when the centurion looked up at Jesus, he spontaneously uttered the words *Truly this was God's Son!*

> **Truly this was God's Son!**
> MATTHEW 27:54 AMP

That is because what he saw was the unleashing of God's amazing, majestic power. The moment Jesus died, there was a rock-shattering earthquake—the mighty force that had been restrained in his body was finally released to defeat death and give eternal life.

The centurion saw the power of God, and so can you today. Allow it to be released in your life, for truly he is God's Son.

Dear God, I can't even begin to imagine the remarkable power you hold. Thank you for expending it for my good and your glory. Amen.

He was shown with great power to be the Son of God by being raised from death.

ROMANS 1:4 GNT

Hearing Your Heart

To say that words are not sufficient to express everything that is inside of you is an amazing understatement. Could you shout it out, you would exhaust your vocal cords before you ever got close to finishing.

> **We do not know what to pray for as we ought, but the Spirit himself intercedes for us with groanings too deep for words.**
>
> ROMANS 8:26 ESV

All of the frustrations and sorrows, of the hopes and dreams—they are so profound and full of emotion that mere words fall hopelessly short of conveying them.

Yet God wants to hear your heart, so he sends his Spirit to examine you—your conscious and subconscious, your innermost thoughts and feelings. And God's Spirit beautifully communicates in his glorious words what is so difficult for you to express.

Dear God, thank you that your Spirit communicates the deep things within me. Thank you that whenever I pray, you really hear me. Amen.

The Father who knows all hearts
knows what the Spirit is saying, for
the Spirit pleads for us believers in
harmony with God's own will.

ROMANS 8:27 NLT

Before You Knew

You don't have to earn God's love. He gives it to you freely. You may sometimes feel as if you need to do something to keep in good standing with him—making a promise or doing some good work—but you don't.

He loved you before you knew he existed. In fact, he loved you before *you* existed.

> **God demonstrates His own love toward us, in that while we were yet sinners, Christ died for us.**
> ROMANS 5:8 NASB

God demonstrated his love for you in a powerful way through the death and resurrection of Jesus. Two thousand years ago, before you knew you needed his love, he was providing it for you.

If you feel lonely or unworthy today, you can cling to this wonderful truth. He loves you. Praise his wonderful name.

Dear God, thank you for loving me even before I knew how much I needed your love. You really are wonderful. Amen.

I trust in your love.
My heart is happy
because you saved me.
PSALM 13:5 NCV

From Wailing to Dancing

Last night you may have had issues that weighed your heart down with sorrow. Yet this morning, God is working to bring you joy.

Mourning and dancing—two responses that are staggeringly different. But God easily alters circumstances that seem hopeless into great reasons for rejoicing.

> **You have turned my mourning into joyful dancing. You have taken away my clothes of mourning and clothed me with joy.**
> PSALM 30:11 NLT

As quickly as God turns night into day, he can change your situation. He can transform your sorrow into jubilation and your cries of pain into hoots of happiness.

What is it that looks dark to you at this moment? Fear not. In just a little while you will be praising him for turning your wailing into dancing.

Dear God, Oh, God—let it be so. You know why I cry, and what would make me dance. May your wonderful, transforming favor shine on me. Amen.

Sing to the Lord, you saints of his; praise his holy name. For his anger lasts only a moment, but his favor lasts a lifetime; weeping may remain for a night, but rejoicing comes in the morning.

PSALM 30:4–5 NIV

Above the Ark

Deep within the temple—in the Most Holy Place—was a beautifully decorated chest called the ark of the Testimony, where God would meet with the high priest.

Interestingly, the word for *ark* in Hebrew means "coffin." Meditate upon that striking picture and poignant principle—God's glory appeared above a coffin.

> **From above the mercy seat, from between the two cherubim that are upon the ark of the Testimony, I will speak intimately with you.**
> EXODUS 25:22 AMP

God's power always rushes in where all hope seems lost. It triumphed over the grave when Jesus was resurrected, and it does wonders for you as well.

Whatever dreams have died for you, God will show you his glory above it. He will speak intimately with you and give you great hope.

Dear God, thank you for bringing life back to my dreams. I praise you for your astounding power and glory that always give me hope. Amen.

Here I am in the place of worship, eyes
open, drinking in your strength and glory. In
your generous love I am really living at last!
My lips brim praises like fountains.

PSALM 63:2–3 MSG

Perfect Peace

Have you ever tried to help someone with a task, only to be told that you were doing it wrong? You were doing your best, yet because it was not the way the other person would do it, it wasn't "right."

> **You keep him in perfect peace whose mind is stayed on you, because he trusts in you. Trust in the LORD forever.**
> ISAIAH 26:3–4 ESV

People often treat God the same way. He has an amazing plan for each of us, yet we still try to wrestle the control from him. He provides his best for us, yet we question and complain because he isn't doing it our way.

Don't miss God's wonderful peace today by choosing your own plans over his. He will give perfect peace to you when you trust him and how he does things.

Dear God, please forgive me for choosing my plans over yours and complaining. Thank you for your perfect plans and perfect peace. Amen.

He has done everything well!

MARK 7:37 HCSB

Why It Happened

It was the same question every time: *Who did wrong?* If the man had been born blind, then someone's mistake must have caused it. Yet Jesus set the disciples straight. It happened so that God's power could be shown.

> **So the power of God could be seen in him.**
> JOHN 9:3 NLT

You may be wondering today why something is happening to you. Though you have prayed, the problem continues. You may even wonder, *What did I do to deserve this?*

This has not happened because of some wrong you have done. Rather, it is because God wants to show his power in you. He will open your eyes, like the blind man's, to his mighty power, and you will see God.

Dear God, I look forward to seeing your power in this situation. Thank you that this is so your glory will be shown. Amen.

**God, order up your power;
show the mighty power you
have used for us before.**

PSALM 68:28 NCV

An Answer Is Coming

There is such a sweetness and benefit to seeking God in the morning. By starting your day with the Bible and prayer, you open yourself to a conversation with him throughout the day.

> **In the morning, O LORD, you hear my voice; in the morning I lay my requests before you and wait in expectation.**
> PSALM 5:3 NIV

It is important to go to God with more than requests and longings. Go to him with a hearing heart. How often do you go to God with the simple intent of listening?

Certainly, there are things you have been asking him about. And his answer is coming to you—that is sure. This morning, listen quietly to your God and wait in expectation for his wondrous reply. His answer is coming—so don't miss it.

Dear God, thank you for hearing me. I want to hear you. Speak straight to my heart, O Lord. I wait in eager expectation. Amen.

I will listen [with expectancy] to
what God the Lord will say, for He
will speak peace to His people.

PSALM 85:8 AMP

Wrestling With Time

This morning, are you crying out, *How long, O Lord?* Most things are endurable as long as you know you will soon have relief. Yet when you have no idea when or if your circumstance will have a resolution, it can be discouraging.

How long, O Lord?
PSALM 13:1 NKJV

You are not only dealing with your situation, but you are also wrestling with the uncertainties of time. Everything could change in a minute or endure interminably.

Be patient. Your God hears you and is the master of both time and your situation. Though you do not know how long it will last, he does. And your waiting will not last one second longer than is necessary.

Dear God, my time is in your hands—and I trust you. It is hard to wait, but worth it knowing that you are handcrafting my future. Amen.

**Look on me and answer, O Lord my God.
Give light to my eyes.**
Psalm 13:3 niv

Searchable Secrets

The mind cannot even begin to conceive all that God knows concerning the construction of the world and everything in it. He says that if you call to him, he will show you.

Amazingly, as you spend time with God, he starts awakening you to things you never even thought to think about. He gives you insights into yourself and other people that are unfathomable without his guidance and teaching.

> **Call to Me and I will answer you and show you great and mighty things, fenced in and hidden, which you do not know.**
> JEREMIAH 33:3 AMP

He also reveals himself to you—the greatest and most wonderful of all knowledge.

Call upon the Lord today, and listen intently to his answer. Surely he will show you great secrets that you will love to know.

Dear God, I listen intently to all you have to share with me. Please teach me all the mighty hidden things I do not know. Amen.

It is the LORD who gives wisdom; from him come knowledge and understanding.

PROVERBS 2:6 GNT

Openhearted

As the Israelites settled into the Promised Land, God instructed them to do something quite shocking. At the end of every seven years, they were to cancel all debts.

Also during that seventh year, they were to put down their tools and relax. It was to be a year of rest from both toil and obligations.

> **Always be generous, open purse and hands, give to your neighbors in trouble, your poor and hurting neighbors.**
> DEUTERONOMY 15:11 MSG

Why? Because God wanted the Israelites to understand that everything they had came from him. And so, knowing his openheartedness toward them, they should likewise be benevolent with others.

God is a giving God, and he wants his people to be generous as well. Today, be openhearted with those who are in need around you.

Dear God, I know that everything I have comes from you. Help me to see others' needs so that I can be as generous as you would. Amen.

Give to them freely
and unselfishly, and
the LORD will bless you
in everything you do.

DEUTERONOMY 15:10 GNT

Moments of Peace
for the Morning

Blessed are those who have learned to acclaim you, who walk in the light of your presence, O LORD.

PSALM 89:15 NIV